CW00541879

ECKINGTON AND THE FIRST WORLD WAR

SOLDIERS AND THEIR FAMILIES

WHAT HAPPENED NEXT

Elaine Chambers

Copyright ©Elaine Chambers

All rights reserved.

No part of this publication may be reproduced, stored in a retrieval system or transmitted in any form or by any means, without the prior permission in writing of the publisher. Neither may it be otherwise circulated in any form of binding or cover other than that in which it is published and without a similar condition including this condition being imposed on the subsequent purchaser.

Elaine Chambers has asserted her right under The Copyright, Designs and Patents Act, 1988 to be identified as the author of this work.

ISBN 978-1-5272-6121-1

Printed and bound in Great Britain
Typeset and cover design by Anna Richards

Dedicated to the People of Eckington
Then, Now and in the Future
Remembering the Sacrifices made

Thanks

To the Eckington Town Team, in particular Chairman, Margaret Fry without which the WW1 Projects would not have got underway, and to members of the Eckington Town Team

To the National Heritage Lottery Fund for their support of the two projects with finance and oversight

To Don Jones for his research and leadership of the WW1 memorial services and Parish church (St Peter and St Paul, Eckington) activities. Especial thanks to Don and Hazel Jones, local Scouts and Brownies for the WW1 Soldiers installation

To local historians Simon Goodwin, Richard Godley, David Nightingale, John Redfern, Kath Murphy, Philip Staton and Linda Taylor of Mosborough History Society, John Tipper and the Barlborough Heritage Centre

To James Clark, WW1 and re-enactment specialist and David King, of the Pro Patria Museum for their input to many aspects of both projects

To the Eckington Reminiscence Group for local information, feedback and support

To the Derbyshire Archives at Matlock and their staff and the Local Studies section at Chesterfield Library for their help and in particular the support of Kester Savage. To Eckington Library for their resources

To the Mercia Regiment (successor to Sherwood Foresters) history team

To the family informants Debbie Hyde (Lund), Ian Marshall (Walker), Mandy Price (Cartlidge), Olive Newton (Robinson), Yvonne Anderson (Heptinstall) and John Redfern (Redfern) and David Nightingale (Nightingale). Bessie Harrop, Anne Joule and John Hinchliffe for significant local background information

To the administrators of and contributors to the Facebook Groups Mosborough History, Eckington Old and New, Natural Eckington and Eckington Parish TV

To John Rose for material on Douglas Wells and work on WW1 projects

To Paul Burdett, photographer and sound and video recorder

To David Grayson, CBE, writer and native of Eckington for support with the writing of this book

To Joy Wale, for her assistance with reviewing the Eckington, Staveley and Woodhouse Express

To Dennis Askham, historian and photographer

Peter O'Driscoll, historian and photgrapher.

Elaine (Lainy) Chambers Rodger was born in Sheffield and returned there in 2016 after many years living away pursuing her career in health management. Now living almost astride the Sheffield/North East Derbyshire border she looks to Eckington as her local community. The Parish Church's World War 1 commemorative work provided a route to a long- standing aspiration to visit the war graves of Northern France and Belgium where her maternal grandfather, Arthur Harding Seddon, had served as a groom to the war horses of the Tank Regiment. The 2018 trip organised by the church inspired further interest in the lives of Eckington people in the war and beyond. The interest fitted with Eckington Town Team's ambition for a further WW1 community project. This is Lainy's first book, hopefully not her last.

Leslie Fry (grandfather of Bill Fry),
WW1 groom on his captain's horse

History is not just about the great leaders and the big, national and international events. History is also about the daily lives of families and communities.

Lainy has produced a very thoughtful and highly readable account of the men from Eckington who made the ultimate sacrifice during World War I; but also about the impact on their families and the community they left behind, both during and after WW1.

Anyone who comes from the area will be fascinated by the wealth of details uncovered. I had no idea, for example, that the Suffragette leader Sylvia Pankhurst was prosecuted at the old Renishaw Magistrates' Court at the end of the war. Reading "Eckington and the First World War: Soldiers and their Families - What Happened Next," I recognised many family names of people I was at primary and junior school with it. Bessie Lund, the daughter of one of Eckington's war dead: Harry Lund, was a teacher with my mother at Camms School. I remember Miss Wells, a cousin of another local war hero: Douglas Wells, as a regular guest at my grandparents' parties when I was growing up. I suspect all of us with roots in Eckington will be able to make similar connections to the individuals and families quoted in the book.

It feels particularly poignant to be writing this foreword, one hundred years after the end of the Spanish flu epidemic, as we confront the coronavirus. Once again, our political leaders tell us, we are at war – only this time, the war is against a virulent epidemic. Let the tales of selflessness and sacrifice and endurance from a hundred years ago, inspire us again.

David Grayson CBE

The First World War took place over a century ago; the armistice was signed on the 11th November, 1918 after a 4 year period when an estimated 17 Million soldiers and civilians were killed around the world. It has left its mark on the world in many ways, some positive and some not, including military strategy, statecraft, health, and nationhood. It has left behind memorials and memories, now passed on to later generations through photos, letters, diaries, books and stories. The town of Eckington and the surrounding civic parish in North East Derbyshire are typical of other places in the UK, in having lost many men in that war, and remembering them with love and gratitude down the generations.

In 1914 the Civic Parish of Eckington covered the town itself and Renishaw, Spinkhill, Ridgeway Marsh Lane, the hamlet of Gleadless, Halfway and Mosborough and had a population of 12,400 people, with a further 4,200 living in nearby Killamarsh. Almost 400 soldiers from this area are thought to have died, 262 are named on the 8 local war memorials (Research: Simon Goodwin). Some names have recently been added to the Marsh Lane Memorial when it underwent restoration. These men were listed as 'missing' at the time, and their families could not accept the near certainty of their deaths, holding on to hope that they would return. This is also likely to apply in Eckington. The Civic Parish has memorials in all of the old wards, some of which (Mosborough and Halfway) were reassigned from North East Derbyshire to Sheffield in a major local authority boundary change in the late 1960s. Some of these communities, in particular Renishaw and Mosborough, have done their own historical research work since 2014 and collaboration between local groups and historians has been very helpful to the Eckington research. This book follows on from a shorter one made available for the centenary of the signing of the armistice on the 11th November 1918. It concentrates on Eckington, on the families of those 85 men whose names appear on the Eckington memorial and on the effect of the war on the lives of the people of Eckington during the years 1914 onwards into the early 1920s.

THE PROJECTS

In 2014 Eckington was awarded funding from the Heritage Lottery Fund (now the National Heritage Lottery Fund) for a project to help local people including schoolchildren to understand the First World War (WW1), especially as it was experienced by the soldiers who served in it. A very popular feature of this project, which has now passed into the town's folk memory, was the trench experience, with a replica dug out, lined with wood, with smoke and typical sound effects set up in a vacant shop in the centre of the town. James Clark, an expert on First World War re-enactment was volunteered to help with stories and sample uniform and kit. The trench experience and the James Clark's talks and re-enactments were recorded with photographs and videos.

Work went on in local schools, including Camms and Eckington Junior Schools, to produce material which was age-appropriate to help the children understand the WW1 experience. The Parish Church set up a display in a side-chapel, including battlefield maps, war diaries, and photographs of local soldiers in action in the pivotal battle of St Quentin Canal from 29th September to 10th October, 1918. The Sherwood Foresters (more properly the Nottinghamshire and Derbyshire Regiment), to which many of the Eckington soldiers belonged, had played a significant part in this alongside other British, Australian and American soldiers. The research work on soldiers named on the Eckington memorial had matched 78 of the 85 with national records, now available through internet search web-sites provided by the Commonwealth War Graves Commission (https://cwgc. org) and others such as Ancestry and Find My Past, had provided their dates of death and other details. The Parish Church held a memorial service for each of these 78, starting with the first death, of Private George Smith, 3rd Battalion York and Lancashire Regiment, on the 7th March 1915. Private Smith's burial place, St. Andrew's Cemetery, Jesmond,

Newcastle-upon Tyne would suggest that he died whilst in training. The last individual death commemorated was that of Lance Corporal Leonard Holmes, King's Own Yorkshire Light Infantry (KOYLI), who died of typhoid fever, following influenza, aged 20 in Cologne on the 3rd June 1919. A final service was held in church on the 28th June 2019, the anniversary of the signing of the Treaty of Versailles, for the men who could not be traced at the time of the original research. William Andress, George B Frith, and possibly Albert P York (Yorke on memorial) had been identified at around the time the final service took place as a result of further research and families coming forward, leaving Albert Barber, John E Davison, William C Greaves and David Hopkinson untraced and Richard Davis (or Davies) not conclusively traced as had been recorded in the first booklet. As each service was held, names were added to the replica memorial and records placed in a memorial book. Several families were able to attend the services for their relatives, some coming forward as a result of publicity of the project in The Sheffield Star. This included the family of Sergeant Harry Lund, MM (Military Medal), one of the families written up later in this booklet.

In August 2018, the Eckington Town Team had secured another National Heritage Lottery Fund grant for a further project, World War 1: Eckington Soldiers and their Families, What Happened Next. This funding covered a new work programme from 2018 to 2020 involving audio recordings of local people to be available to the community in the

future,★ events around the centenary of the armistice on 11th November 2018 and a book. The Remembrance Day Service, as every year since 1920 when the memorial was dedicated, involved a march from the West End, West Street, Eckington to the Parish Church of St Peter and St Paul for current and ex service personnel, with a service in the church followed by a silent remembrance of the fallen and the laying of wreaths. For the service in 2018 scouts, cubs, brownies and members of the congregation came forward with a replica soldier for each of the 85 men named on the memorial. This very well attended service was videoed as part of the community archive, established by Natural Eckington. (http:naturaleckington.uk/)

The Eckington Town Team put on a short drama in the local Civic Centre again with the help of James Clark, our WW1 re-enactment specialist, to bring to life aspects of the war years locally, from enlistment to the effect of deaths of young soldiers on the community, and the mingled joy and sadness of the announcement of the armistice. David King, who has a collection of WW1 costumes and artefacts, helped with the production.

*Recordings will be available via a U-turns listening point to be established in Eckington.

Research has continued throughout the period of the second grant. Families have been encouraged to come forward through word of mouth, the Eckington Town Team's newsletter, a display in the local library, use of local web-sites, including Eckington Old and New and Natural Eckington. In addition to the Lund and Morton families who were identified from the original project, a further 7 local families are presented in the book. Their stories illustrate various aspects of the wartime experience and its aftermath.

The research with the Lund family uncovered a newspaper account of the dedication of the Eckington War Memorial on 27th June 1920 with an ecumenical (multi-faith) service led by the Rector throughout the war years, the Rev W R Hewson. A service of rededication is planned for the centenary weekend of the original one. In advance of that, the monument is being restored to its original state, including the 20 names of lives sacrificed in WW2 and the 2 in the Falklands War.

Records in the Derbyshire Archives at Matlock have been especially illuminating. In particular the discovery of the original plan for the Eckington War Memorial. Apart from the striking effect of the detail and delicate colouring, the fact that it was signed off within only three weeks of the signing of the armistice shows how dear those who died were to the community to which they belonged.

Chesterfield Libraries Local Studies Department has also provided much material for this book through its archived copies of the Eckington, Staveley and Woodhouse Express. This weekly newspaper was published from the late 19th Century until 1935, heavily supported by advertising, often cleverly related to what was happening in the war years and after. It also functioned as the social media of its day, with up to date local information on people and events. The column relating to Eckington bore the title 'Eckington Gossip'. During the War Years it announced the upcoming leave of soldiers, no doubt so that they could make best use of their limited time back home, and the award of medals and decorations. Less happily, it reported casualties, men taken prisoner and deaths. It covered the work of the community to support war efforts; fund-raising, holding services, and taking care of widows. Outside of the Gossip column, the editorials were often wise, forward looking and informative. Local and national events were covered including strikes, industrial issues, food shortages, and politics in particular the 1918 election.

STORY OF A DECADE 1914-1924
War years 1914 to 1917

1914 Key events and dates

4th August	War declared by UK on Germany
23 August	Battle of Mons and subsequent retreat
10 October	Fall of Antwerp
19 October to	
22 November	First Battle of Ypres, concluding with establishment of fixed trench lines along western front
16 December	Bombardment of Scarborough by German Navy
25 December	Unofficial Christmas truce reported in some areas of Western Front

Life in the area of South Yorkshire and North East Derbyshire covered by the Eckington, Staveley and Woodhouse Express was not idyllic in July 1914. There had been a death of a young boy, Daniel Nightingale, age 7, in Eckington and in the larger area, a disaster at Wharncliffe Colliery with a large death toll which had led to an enquiry. Summer had brought a church outing in Eckington and a sale of work at the Wesleyan church in aid of better arrangements for registration of weddings. Prophetically, there were also thunderstorms in which rain 'fell in torrents'.

War was declared by the UK government on Germany on the 4th August. Thunderous headlines appeared in the paper, together with a European map, soon to become very familiar in Britain as they followed the course of the war, and for some, the whereabouts of their sons, husbands and brothers.

The paper was quick to start a column, the War Day by Day, starting with the invasion of neutral Luxemburg, the mobilisation of the French army, and the cancellation of European trips. By the middle of the month, the Prince of Wales had established a fund for the 'alleviation of distress' and a National Day of Prayer had been called.

By late August, the news was of Belgian refugees, some of whom came to Britain. Money was raised in many

THE EXPRESS, SATURDAY, AUGUST 8, 1914

communities to help them. Territorial soldiers were being mobilised. The Derbyshire Miners Association paid tribute to the Colliery Owners for providing allowances to the families of those whose breadwinners had left to train and fight.

The first casualties were reported on in September, by which time they numbered just over 5,000. What was striking was how large the proportion of 'missing' was in relation to those known to have been killed or wounded. Nevertheless, the war did not completely dominate; there was still space to report a fashionable Eckington wedding, the opening of the football season with Eckington Athletic beating Mosborough Town 2-1 and the opening of a new

Salvation Army Citadel on West Street. However, the September and October papers bore news of the course of the war and on enlistment (see Enlistment section). In October, the paper invited readers who received letters from men on active service to send them to the Express office with a view to publication. This continued through the war, together with reports from relatives.

Eckington had a possible first casualty in October 1914: Albert P Yorke, the last WW1 name on the memorial could be Albert P York. There is no report in the local newspaper but this may be explained by the remarriage and re-location of his widow in the years between his death and the erection of the memorial. Details are in the table below.

Eckington turned its attention to supporting the war in whatever ways it could. An ambulance brigade was to be raised, a rifle club formed, a local relief fund and committee set up and the first dance to raise money for the National War Fund was held. In November a muffled peal of the church bells was made in memory of the National casualties. In December an entertainment was held at the Picture House in aid of the Belgian Refugees. Local children did what they could to help; the pupils of Camms School gave their pennies to buy wool which the girls knitted into mufflers, mittens and cuffs for soldiers. These were sent to the Queen and a thank you letter was received from a lady in waiting. The Infant Department of Eckington School also knitted for soldiers that autumn.

The troops were all provided with Princess Mary tin boxes of comforts. Distribution proved challenging as more boxes were required for all the troops now serving. In consequence, some were delivered in the New Year with a revised message from the Palace.

The general fear of invasion of England was heightened shortly before Christmas when the Yorkshire coast was bombarded. Reflecting on the Festival of Christmas, the Eckington, Staveley and Woodhouse Express wrote:

'This year the Christmas season comes upon us when our hearts are not tuned for rejoicing...'

Surname	First Names	Date of Death
York (Yorke on memorial)★ Corporal 79382, 2nd Battn KOYLI Husband of Nellie Davis (formerly York) 70 Lorden's Hill, Dinnington, Rotherham	Albert Percy	31 October

★Possible identification not in previous booklet

1915 Key events and dates

18th February	German navy commences submarine blockade of UK
22nd April	First use of gas as a weapon on the Western Front by German army (Allies used later)
25th April	Allied landing commence in Dardenelles (Galliopoli)
7th May	Lusitania sunk by German submarine in Atlantic
25th May	Formation of coalition Government in the UK under PM H. H. Asquith
31 May	First Zeppelin raid on London (earlier one on Great Yarmouth)
5th October	British and French troops land in Salaika (Northern Greece)
19th December	Sir Douglas Haig replaces Sir John French as Commander in Chief of the British Expeditionary Force on the Western Front. Evacuation of Gallipoli commences.

The New Year arrived, with quite a number of serving men home on leave. Tea was served for them in the Wesleyan schoolroom. Toys were provided for their children and variety entertainment followed in the Assembly Rooms. Christmas services were well attended with more than 200 communicants at the Parish Church on Christmas Day. A separate set of three services was held in January for intercessions (prayers) for the end of the War. A number of soldiers attended. Wives and families of serving soldiers had begun to experience financial difficulties. The Eckington Parochial Relief Committee agreed to give them an advance from the Prince of Wales Fund pending receipt of the support they were promised from the Government's War Office.

In March the first death of an Eckington man was reported in the paper. Pte Wm Smith (recorded on the war memorial as George Smith). He was a regular soldier, who had been recalled for service and gone to train in Newcastle upon Tyne where he became ill and died. He was the son of Mrs Emma Pilkington, 3 St John's Hill, Eckington, who had two younger sons, both serving in the forces at the time of their older half-brother's death. George/ William Smith was 43, had served in the 3rd Yorks and Lancs Regiment for 23 years, including service in the South

African (Boer) War, with 7 bars and 2 medals. Afterwards he worked as a labourer for Mr Mason, a mason of Eckington. In 1914, he re-joined the regiment as a reservist. After his death in a Newcastle's Armstrong Hospital on the 7th March 1915, he was given a military funeral and was buried in St Andrew's and Jesmond Cemetery in Newcastle.

More cheerfully, Pte Wm Lingard of the 6th Sherwood Foresters Company writes on behalf of Eckington lads J Huckles, P Marper, J Nightingale on March 23:

"Well we are all in good health after being in trenches 4-5 days in companies 24 hours at a time within 60 yards of the German trenches. Now at rest camp for a week or two - 5/6 miles away. Most are billeted in houses with French families who do their best for us. Give our best wishes to our friends in Eckington".

All four are thought to have survived the War. J Nightingale is heard of again in the paper in 1918 (see Nightingale Family). Letters and postcards were exchanged with great regularity between serving soldiers and their family and friends (see Marshall and Cartlidge Families in particular). Cards and ready formatted letters were often used, some beautiful and elaborate.

Eckington friends Arthur Riley and James Silvers were not so fortunate, becoming the first two Eckington lads to be killed (see Enlistment). These men and Alfred Greaves, a Marine, were casualties of the Gallipoli Campaign. Pte R S Crisp of the Royal Rifles, living at High Street Eckington was reported as having been killed in action in France in the early summer. He was a reservist, who prior to his call-up had been a rural postman on the Eckington Troway route. Surprisingly, his name does not appear on the Eckington Memorial.

The first Eckington man to die in France who is memorialised on the Eckington Memorial was George Hutchinson who died on the 16th June 1915, aged 19. Other deaths and wounded casualties were reported throughout the year. At least four of these men were married, and four were over 30. Herbert Ferguson the eldest at 48. James Oates was 39 and left a widow and five children. This probably reflects the nature of the fighting force in 1915 – with proportionately more regular solders and reservists.

Deaths and injuries continued in the Dardanelles during the rest of the year. Conditions were poor. Just as in France, there was trench warfare with heavy shelling and the danger of snipers, always on the lookout for heads above the trenches and good

shots, as Thomas Farrell wrote to a friend on 1st August, days before he was killed. Lance Corporal G W Kirk was also killed in the Dardanelles that August and Pte William Turton, injured.

At home, an Eckington tribute was held for the fallen on the 23rd October. The Eckington and Renishaw sections of the Home Guard took part and marched from the West End Hotel to the Parish Church headed by the Eckington United Prize Band.

Surname	First Names	Date of Death
Smith	George	7th March
Riley	Arthur	4th June
Silvers	James	4th June
Hutchinson	George	16th June
Greaves	Alfred	15th July
Munday	William	7th August
Artherton or Arthurton	Sidney	9th August
Farrell	Thomas	9th August
Kirk	George Whinfrey	21st August
Nicholson	John William	27th September
Doxey	Isaac Henry	1st October
Oates	James	4th October
Ferguson	Herbert	5th October
Partridge	Alfred Thomas	9th December
Taylor	Wilfred	16th December

1916 Key events and dates

February	Military Service Act introduces conscription for unmarried men 18-41
24th April	Start of Easter Rising in Ireland
25th May	Military Service Act amended and conscription introduced for married men
31st May	Battle of Jutland: naval engagement in North Sea
1st July	Battle of the Somme commences. 60,000 British casualties on first day, including 20,000 killed and 40,000 wounded. Continues until the 13 November
15th September	First use of tanks during attacks on village of Flers - Courcelette on Somme
28 September	First bombing raids on London
December	Herbert Asquith resigns as PM and is replaced by David Lloyd George

The New Year started with the death of an Eckington soldier in France, Ernest Pattison on the 1st January. It was time of heavy casualties with a high number of wounded, although no more recorded deaths occurred until the beginning of March. Enlistment continued and was praised and encouraged. Two miners, Henry Levick and Frank Anderson enlisted in the Royal Scottish Fusiliers in February. In parallel, conscription was introduced that month (see enlistment). Pte W H Harrison had enlisted some months earlier. His parents had been surprised that he was accepted as he was 33 and had only one eye. He was sent to France as a messenger where he died

in an accident in June. There had been contention about who should perform the medicals for men enlisting, military authorities or civilian personnel, as the former had an obvious interest.

The 1st July 1916 was the first day of the Battle of the Somme and the day of the highest number of casualties in WW1, with almost 40,000 wounded and 20,000 dead. The Eckington, Staveley and Woodhouse Express was overwhelmed with reports from families of their dead and injured and promised to cover them as soon as it could. Enoch Jones, Reginald (George Elgie) Ward, Alfred Hadfield died that day and Herbert Colin Ditcher on the 3rd July. A memorial service was held for Enoch Jones at his local church where he had been a teacher. The laboratory staff at Staveley Coal and Iron expressed their deepest sympathy of the loss of their former colleague, Colin Ditcher. There were also a number of local men wounded. Two more deaths occurred in August: Lance Corporal Fred Hadfield, a married man of 7 Gosber Street and Pte William Waring, a Somme death as he is commemorated on the Thiepval Memorial to the missing. He had been a miner at Markham Colliery prior to enlistment. Captain Edgar Parker was also killed in France. He is not commemorated on the Eckington Memorial as he was no longer living in Eckington but had been secretary of the Eckington Silver Band. The names of six Eckington men were eventually added to the Thiepval Memorial.

The Prince of Wales Relief Committee had now become the War Relief Committee. The Eckington Branch was chaired by Mr T Greensmith. There was an understanding that the local branches would ensure that the dependents of any soldiers killed would receive their rent and an allowance for 6 months. The State would take over at that point. Other matters were becoming more formalised too. Volunteer duties and status was defined, with eligibility from age 17, a green-grey (not khaki) uniform and the remit of special constables who were to be linked to the military as necessary. In October, there was a new rule for earlier closing of shops although it is not clear whether this was because supplies were becoming more limited or to do with lighting as a night-time blackout had been introduced early in the war.

The length of the war and lack of conclusive success in battle was becoming wearisome.

By the autumn conscription had become a fact of life as were the local tribunals which considered exemptions, short or longer term. Relationships between the military and the tribunals were not always harmonious. Voluntary enlistment was still allowed and praiseworthy. Mr Fred Mills, a member of the Parish Council joined the colours in

September, having worked hard to get others to enlist since the outbreak of war. The clerk was instructed to write to him to convey the Council's best wishes and expressing the hope that he would have a safe return.

It is not clear whether shortage of men affected the Eckington Wesleyan Football Team but the start to their season was dire. They lost 11-1 to Mosborough away. It did rather better later in the season, drawing 2-2 with Swallownest. Boys were increasingly expected to step up to replace brothers and fathers at war. The Eckington District Schools Committee reduced the age of compulsory schooling to 13 in November so they could help with farming. Compulsory evening education was introduced nationally.

There were several more military deaths in the autumn, the last being that of Edmund Bruce Hollingworth on the 26th October. Unusually, there was an elaborate military funeral for him in Eckington. This was partly because he had died in England, in hospital at Chatham after an unsuccessful operation for wounds sustained in France and on account of being the youngest brother to Maynard Hollingworth, the agent of Sir George Sitwell. The funeral set out from Northwood House on the Renishaw Hall estate with the coffin borne on a dray belonging to the estate. Bruce's four brothers attended, two

having returned from Canada to do so. The coffin was borne into church by soldiers from the Sherwood Foresters. The congregation was large, including many estate staff. Bruce had worked briefly on the estate after leaving school before enlisting at the age of only 17. He was 20 at the time of his death.

In November, Mrs Mary Wells, widow of Joseph Wells (see Wells Family) died after a short illness at the age of 90. She was closely associated with St Marks Church, Mosborough which the Wells had founded but was also a patron of Eckington Church. She was buried in the old churchyard next to the church alongside her husband. Many members of her family attended the funeral. In all four of her children outlived her, including Sophia living close by in Elmwood House.

For an all too brief period of three and a half months, including Christmas, there were no military deaths of Eckington men between late October and February 1917. An anonymous donor provided Christmas boxes to a value of 2s 6d each (value £10 at 2020 prices) to all dependents of soldiers and sailors in Eckington, an estimated 700-900 recipients. A whist drive had been held at the Institute early in December for comforts for the men themselves.

The Eckington Institute hosted regular indoor events for wounded men throughout the period. The building is still standing; it is now known as the Corner Playhouse, High Street, Eckington, and is home to the City Players.

Surname	First Names	Date of Death
Pattison	Ernest	1st January
Bristow	Henry	7th March
Woodthorpe	William Albert	9th May
Robinson	Arthur Harold	10th May
Harrison	William Henry	9th June
Hadfield	Alfred	1st July
Jones	Enoch (Enock)	1st July
Ward	Reginald (George Elgie)	1st July
Ditcher (Kitcher)	Herbert Colin	3rd July
Waring	William	13th August
Hadfield	Fred	21st August
Hutchinson	Ernest	8th September
Fidler	Edwin	15th September
Haddock	Alfred J	16th September
Smedley	Samuel George	26th September
Crouch	Fred	29th September
Nightingale	Arthur	7th October
Hollingworth	Edmund Bruce	26th October

1917 Key events and dates

February	Germany declares unrestricted submarine warfare
March	German Army withdraws to pre-prepared defensive positions on Hindenburg Line
6th April	USA declares war on Germany
9th April	Easter Monday. First day of the Battle of Arras
15th May	Marshall Petain appointed as French Commander in Chief after turbulent month for French forces
31st July	Opening day of the third Battle of Ypres, more commonly referred to as Passchendaele, which continues until October
1st-3rd September	Battle of Riga. Riga taken by German Army although Russian 12th Army retreated intact
9th December	British troops capture Jerusalem
15th December	Armistice signed between Russian Bolsheviks and the central powers (Germany)

By 1917, war had become almost routine. Fighting was intense on both the Western and Eastern Fronts in Europe and elsewhere. On the Home Front there were fierce air activities including Zeppelin raids over London and one over the Lincolnshire coast. The Eckington, Staveley and Woodhouse Express would commonly carry 20 or more Heroes of the War in every weekly edition, now almost invariably accompanied by a head and shoulders photograph of each man. Sadly, most are very indistinct. The Eckington Burial Board proposed free interment for fallen soldiers (a number died after being invalided home). It considered, but rejected, the idea of a separate area within the cemetery , so that the war dead, including those with headstones provided by the Commonwealth War Graves Commission, are to be found throughout the older part of the cemetery.

Shortage of manpower at home was becoming a major issue. Volunteers were sought for home defence. Boys were being recruited for agricultural work; Eckington District Schools Committee agreed that they would 'again reduce' the age for compulsory education to 12. There were also advertisements for enrolling for National Service at home. Food was also a growing concern with the Government calling for a voluntary reduction in consumption in April. Other shortages were newsprint and in what was a particularly cold winter, fuel. Whilst the end of the war was not in sight, provision for its casualties was now a growing concern. These included pensions for the disabled, re-settlement of the disabled for work and support for widows and children. The war was very costly in this and other ways. The public were constantly urged to contribute through War Loans, with strident adverts in the lead up to each War Loan deadline, such as the one on 6th February, 1917. Repayment took its time, the final WW1 War loans were only paid off in 2015: https://www.bbc.co.uk/news/business-303006579.

There were sad losses in Eckington at home and in the fighting. At home, two young siblings died of diphtheria, a dangerous scourge of the time. Two deaths at the front were of men of only

20. Sergeant Albert Rippon, from Littlemore, had been the youngest sergeant in his Battalion, 1st Sherwood Foresters when he died on the 4th March. Sergeant Leonard Butler, of the 12th Brigade Royal Field Artillery died on the 13th April. His captain wrote that 'he was always such a good boy and cheerful throughout all our hardship'.

Leonard Butler's death was the first of a number of Eckington military deaths that spring and early summer. A further 16 deaths occurred before end of July, including Eckington's highest ranking casualty, Major Frederick Vickers, 15th Battalion, Sherwood Foresters and Second Lieutenant Douglas Henry Wells, 5th Battalion, Yorks and Lancaster Regiment (see Wells Family) . Vickers, a married man, had served in the South African (Boer) War, offered his services for WW1. Re-enlisting as Lieutenant he was rapidly promoted to major. He had been hospitalised for shell shock and had only just returned to duty at the time of his death. A family wedding in July was a very constrained event out of respect for his widow.

Fundraising events continued through the summer and also the provision of a practical support – an entertainment for wounded men in the grounds of the Rectory. These men were recovering in Sheffield hospitals.

The afternoon's entertainment included a cricket match between the ladies (Captain Miss M Taylor) and the gentlemen.

The autumn saw German successes on both the East and Western Fronts and again, heavy losses of men. Six Eckington men were killed in September and October. The first was Joseph William Shaw, a mason at Renishaw Hall. Then three men for whom there was a memorial service in the Parish Church at the end of October; Sergeant Frank Tees Humphries, Pte Lancelot Ramsden and Pte Richard Davies. The first two were well known to the church as regular attenders. Frank Humphries lived on Church Street and was a bell-ringer. One of the saddest deaths was that of Reuben Silvers, aged 19. He had joined the Kings Own Scottish Borders

following in the steps of his brother James, killed in action in action in 1915. Reuben had only been in France for one month before his death.

In November, the Army Council turned its thoughts towards Christmas and made arrangements with voluntary organisations to provide every member of the British Expeditionary Force with a plum pudding. Families were not to send them (thus saving home-based supplies) although other gifts were encouraged. In early December a concert took place at the Institute in aid of the Soldiers and Sailors Comfort Fund.

November and December seemed happier months. On the battlefront, British troops captured Jerusalem on the 15th December, bringing to an end the thundering of guns around the holy places of Jerusalem and Nazareth. There were quite a few serving men home on leave in Eckington. Then came the sad news of the death of Sergeant Harry Lund on 28th December (see Lund family). It was a private sadness, known only to family and friends as it was not reported in the press until January.

Surname	First Names	Date of Death
Milner	T Sidney	13th February
State	Richard	18th February
Rippon	Albert	4th March
Butler	Leonard	13th April
Vickers	Frederick	21st April
Pattison	Joseph	26th April
Herring	James Alfred	28th April
Hartley	George William	29th April
Kirby	Wilfred	3rd May
Wells	Douglas Henry	3rd May
Hardwick	Harold	5th May
Price	Percy	5th June
El(l)cock	Francis	9th June
Holmes	Herbert	9th June
Andress★ Rifleman 372461 8th Battn London Regiment (Post Office Rifles)	William	7th June Remembered with Honour Vormezeele Enclosure No. 3
Fisher	Charles	18th June
Tagg	Benjamin Haydn	18 June
Greaves	George William Marples	29th June
Brown	John	17th July
Robinson	Simeon	19th July
Shaw	Joseph William	24th September
Humphries	Frank Tees	28th September
Ramsden	Lancelot	28th September
Russon	Benjamin	2nd October
Simmons	Edwin	4th October
Silvers	Reuben	14th October
Davies★★	Richard	27th October
Lund	Harry	28th December

★Not identified in previous booklet   ★★ Identification still unclear

Turning Point 1918

1918 Key events and dates

3rd March	Treaty of Brest-Litovsk between Russia and Germany ends the war on the Eastern Front, releasing large number of German forces for the Western Front
21st March	Kaiserschlacht. Germany launches the first of a series of offensives designed to break the Anglo-French lines prior to the arrival of a large number of American troops. First stage Somme; second stage Arras
1st April	Formation of the RAF (Royal Air Force) with amalgamation of the Royal Flying Corps and Royal Naval Air Service
14th April	Marshall Foch (French) appointed Allied Supreme Commander
23rd April	American Expeditionary Force begins to arrive in France and Belgium
3 August	British Forces land in Northern Russia, following murder of Tsar Nicholas and family by Bolsheviks in mid July
8th August	Allied advances commence with the Battle of Amiens. Start of final 100 days of the war. Described by German High Command as the 'Blackest Day of the German Army'
27 September	British Forces successfully break the Hindenburg Line defences on the Canal du Nord
October	Battles: St Quentin Canal, Beaurevoir, Cambria, Pursuit of Selle
4th November	Battle of the Sambre
11th November	Armistice comes into effect at 11.00am on the Western Front
14th December	British General Election

Babyland Predicts Peace—

In the New Year

In every home where baby has the "comforts" Babyland can provide.

There are 3 Things . .

every British Baby should have:—

A "Babyland" Cot——

for the period when "Nature's ..ft nurse, balmy sleep," is fitting the little one for the battle of life.

A "Babyland" Chair——

to save such a lot of toil and tussle during mother's busy time.

A "Babyland" Carriage

for that "out o' doors life" so essential to baby's health and welfare.

We've a Great Variety

of the above and other "Baby Comforts," at just the prices you want to pay. Won't you come and look round our Showrooms. No obligation to buy just when you call if it's not convenient.

Our ONLY Address is easy to Remember

BABYLAND Ltd.

NINETEEN ANGEL St. **SHEFFIELD**

Five Minutes from BOTH Stations. Cars pass the Door.

If you cannot call, send for CATALOGUE MT? [but a call is best.]

There is a more hopeful tone in the press from the very start of 1918, in the advertisements, the editorials and the copy generally. Peace was however, far from a forgone conclusion at the beginning of the year. The capitulations of the Russians, with the Bolshoviks signing an armistice with the Central Powers at the end of 1917, left the Allies on the Western Front dangerously exposed to the possibility of German troops on the Eastern Front being switched to join their comrades on the Western Front. It was not until April that the USA joined the Allies and the end of that month before the first American troops arrived in Europe. Even then, the battles as the Allies, now including the USA had to fight to break the Hindenburg Line were hard won and took many months.

King George called for a National Day of Prayer in January. It was marked in Eckington in the Parish Church (and no doubt in all the other local churches). Fund raising started the first week in January with a whist drive and dance held in the Eckington Institute in aid of the Soldiers and Sailors Comforts Fund. It continued on with at least one event weekly throughout the year. Sometimes the performers were quite well-known: Eva Rich a well-known soprano in Sheffield at the time, appeared at the Eckington United Methodists at the end of January. Further afield, later in the year, Vesta Tilley appeared at Sheffield Empire Palace. The Parish Council's first meeting of the year was a special meeting to consider a Parliamentary Bill being sought by Sheffield Corporation to run buses to Eckington. The Parish Council gave it their support.

The Eckington Staveley and Woodhouse Express continued to run its Heroes of War feature covering servicemen killed, wounded or gassed, invalided home, taken prisoner, missing. More happily, the district columns including Eckington Gossip, additionally reported those home on leave. These short bulletins now often included how long each man had served and been wounded. At example from 16th March reads: on leave; Pte Albert Jennings, age 25, married, enlisted 1914, wounded 3 times, previously miner. Another on 23rd March: on leave Pte Fred Nightingale, High Street, enlisted soon after outbreak of War, in France nearly 3 years.

In April, following the passing of the 'Representation of the People Act', the paper made the comment on the compilation of the new Voters Roll that people had become so used to filling in forms that they would not find the requirements for this daunting. In May, the paper ran a leader criticising the rise of pacifism in England. Volunteers became more needed at home. At the end of June, an Order In Council was passed making men exempted from Military Service obliged to perform volunteer duties. An ambulance class was started at the Eckington Institute in July.

Through the summer there was a feeling of 'still waiting' but quiet optimism. An editorial wrote of *'Unconquerable France. The irrepressible buoyance of the French people is well illustrated by the fact that it is possible*

for them to discuss the cheerful rumour that the French General Staff anticipates clearing France of the enemy by October.' Sometimes, despite continuing casualties and 'flu, timeless local events took place such as the annual Rectory Garden Party where gentlemen and ladies played a cricket match and the Silver Prize Band played 'a selection'.

A leader in the paper on 5th October read 'great expectations' and acknowledged 'Ten weeks of unexampled effort'. October reported the leave of Pte Wilfred Tomlinson of Peveril Road. Aged only 21 and so close to the end of the War, he was to die after the Armistice in February 1919, one of the last of the Eckington prisoners of war.

In the November papers, there was almost disbelief that peace had finally arrived. There was momentary hesitation and disbelief, but after this was dispelled, the news was greeted with joy and relief. The King sent a message to the British Empire's Fighting Forces and the population looked forward to the return of prisoner of war and soldiers and sailors still at their stations. Amidst all the joy and victorious headlines 'Armageddon Ended', 'Germany Down and Out', 'Submission to the Allies' and 'Drastic Armistice Terms' was a prophetic article expressing the view that peace would not

automatically bring prosperity. The economic future would depend on increased production, well paid workers and financial self-control. The 1920s in the UK was notable for industrial unrest and poor economic decisions at national level.

There were celebrations across the country. In North Derbyshire, once the news could be believed, the bunting came out and the bells were rung. The Rector, Rev W R Hewson recorded in his service book, 'Armistice signed. Hostilities cease. Thanksgiving for Peace'. Celebratory parties were held in some communities, the picture below is of one at Halfway.

Men continued to be needed in Europe. The Services set about the task of recruiting 'The Peace Army' placing advertisements asking men to re-enlist for 2, 3 or 4 years in some regiments – cavalry, guards and tanks. Attractive pay and furloughs (leave).

The General Election dominated the news in December, although polling was light. The coalition headed by Lloyd George was re-elected. North East Derbyshire returned a Liberal, Sir Joseph Stanley Holmes, who served until 1922, when he was ennobled. The Labour candidate, Frank Lee was defeated. The atmosphere was light in the papers with Christmas mirth and cartoons and the review of the year commenting on Germany's dramatic collapse and Foch's decisive strategy.

Surname	First Names	Date of Death
Askew	Joseph	11th March
Dale	Alfred Parks	15th March
Fenton	John	21st March
Nettleship	Arthur	21st March
Rhodes	Albert T	2nd April
Smith	John Thomas	18th April
Pearson	George H	9th May
Barker	James Thomas	20th July
White	James	16th August
Nightingale	Edgar	20th August
Frith★ Pte 5864 1st Battn Leinster Regiment	George B	18th September Remembered with honour Ramieh War Cemetery
Shaw	Henry	27th September
Waddingham	James Herbert	29th September
Clayton	Herbert	7th October
Harper	James Frederick	17th October
Priday	Charles E	11th November
Turner	Harold	27th November

★Not identified in previous booklet

Aftermath 1919-1924

1919 Key events and dates

4th January	Opening of Peace conference in Paris
21st June	The surrendered German Naval Fleet scuttled off Scapa Flow
28th June	The Treaty of Versailles signed by Germany and the Allied Powers
	Other Peace Treaties signed between parties continued until 1923. Treaty of Lausanne Between Ottoman Empire and Allied Powers: French Republic, British Empire, Kingdom of Italy, Empire of Japan, Kingdom of Greece and Kingdom of Romania.

The New Year saw change and new concerns. As usual, it was reflected in the advertisements of the day, with one Barnsley store promoting a Demobilisation Sale (including a fine portrait of Field Marshall Sir Douglas Haig). A little later in the year an advertisement for men's suits declared 'before the war styles won't do.'

There was gratitude for those who had served, now sometimes referred to as the 'Men who won the Peace.' The urge to honour and respect those who had lost their lives was stronger than ever with the Eckington War Recognition Committee giving a copy of the picture 'The Great Sacrifice' to the relatives of the fallen (see p 60).

The names of men discharged from military service start to appear in the paper, an early one being Sgt S W Redfern. These often contained a brief summary of service; how long, whether wounded and where served. Alongside this, men still serving were coming home on leave as before. One of these, Sgt Major John Lee of Northgate who had served in the Irish Rebellion was also particularly valued as he had served as goalkeeper for the 1st Battalion of the Sherwood Foresters. In mid-January, five Eckington men were recorded as discharged: Sgt W Hobbs, Pte T Doxey, Pte George Stevenson and Ptes Sam Bennett and Thomas Wardle from 'behind German lines'. Nationally the Government had decided to maintain a force of 900,000 (higher than the military at the outbreak of war) for a period until they felt Germany did not present a threat.

Meanwhile by February the Paris Peace talks had agreed principles. The scale of its task was appreciated. By early June there was concern at length of time between the signing of the armistice and a peace treaty emerging. By this point in the year, there was at times very little expressed concern about the war; Eckington Gossip for 7th June contained only reports on cricket, a biting dog, a wedding and local deaths. The Peace Treaty was reported to be expected to be signed on the 28th June. In fact it was signed that day, although as the paper would have been sent to press before then, it did not over commit. There was rejoicing in Eckington of the day with the ringing of church bells and bunting out again on some of the houses.

Demobilisation was an issue and with it a concern for unemployment. Fortunately for those returning from military service or who lost employment because they had been involved in the manufacture of such munitions, the Liberal Government before the war had introduced unemployment benefit. This also provided a way of helping people into jobs and of monitoring numbers seeking work. By June 1919 the number of men receiving unemployment benefit was just under one million. There was a special scheme under the Ministry of Labour for the re-settlement of officers and for 'educated men'. Finding employment for disabled discharged men was acknowledged as a particular challenge for which there were also special schemes and a Government subsidy available to employers. In March there were reported to be over half a million women in receipt of unemployment benefit. By late June this had halved, although a marked reluctance to return to domestic service was noticed and this led to an improvement in wages and terms and conditions.

Generally, the Labour force was flexing its muscles in a variety of industries. In Eckington a branch of the Agricultural Labourers and Rural Workers Union was established. A parallel development was the instigation of regular buses between Eckington and Sheffield which would in time increase the range of work possible for local residents.

The housing issue was another longstanding one where after the armistice, people were expecting action. In June the Eckington Parish Council had asked the District Council (the building authority under the Addison Act – see Housing) to erect 50 houses at Eckington, 50 at Mosborough and Halfway, 20 at Gleadless, 20 at Renishaw and 12 at Ridgeway. Sites were to be sought. The houses would not all be additional, some existing houses would be condemned and replaced.

A meeting of the War Memorial Committee reported that £210 of the £580 sought had been raised. The site had been agreed as the green space outside the Parish Church. The design had previously been approved. In June, the French Government had designated 140 battle fields to be preserved, one of these being Thiepval on the Somme. This was of great importance to local residents who had lost family members, who would have been pleased to hear the news that the graves would be available to the general public soon.

In what turned out to be the last accredited WW1 death of an Eckington soldier, the Eckington, Staveley and Woodhouse Express reported the death of Leonard Holmes on the 3rd June 1919, at the age of 19. Lance Corporal Holmes, served in the Kings Own Yorkshire Light Infantry and died of typhoid at Cologne. He had worked at Staveley Iron Works before enlisting. His mother, a widow, lived at 86 High Street Eckington.

Surname	First Names	Date of Death
Tomlinson	Wilfred	3rd February 1919
Holmes	Leonard	3rd June 1919
Barber★	Albert	
Davison★	John E	
Greaves★	William C	
Hopkinson★	David	

★Details and dates of death unknown as at February 2020

1920

The early years of the 1920s were quiet by comparison with the war years. There was activity on the political and industrial front. New trends of greater emancipation of women; new interest in homes and gardens, and the increase in cars and motor cycles and buses can be traced at home.

The first January edition of the Eckington, Staveley and Woodhouse Express started with the customary review of the previous year, noting a New Europe with new states including (Y)Jugo-Slavia with the collapse of the old Austrian Empire, the legacy of anarchy and chaos in Russia, the birth of the League of Nations, the developments in aviation, the first woman member of parliament to take her seat (Viscountess Nancy Astor), the boom in sport. The latter is very evident in the paper throughout 1920 and beyond; there is a great deal of coverage of football (including women's) and cricket. Sport seemed to have replaced war in terms of column inches.

Re-settlement as such proceeded well with the numbers of unemployed nationally down significantly from 1919. Early in the year, the Government was able to claim that 3.5 million ex-servicemen (excluding officers) had been re-settled. However, clearly some thought that life abroad may offer more; a February edition of the paper carried an advertisement for emigration.

Men are wanted for the farm, women for the homes of Canada (Feb 21st 1920 Ed 1144)

Fierce opposition was expressed at all levels to coal nationalisation and there was an electricians' strike.

In June, work started to install the Eckington War Memorial on its designated site on the green space owned by the Parish Council, close to the Parish Church and in front of the White Hart public house. The Memorial itself was ready, but the money for the fencing was outstanding, and possibly remained so as the memorial has never been fenced. Later that month, on Sunday 27th June, the memorial was unveiled in a multi-faith service by Mrs Henry Lund (see commemoration and Lund Family) with its 85 names. There was a major tolling of the bells (Bob Minor and Bob Major) which were half muffled for respect.

The spirit of philanthropy and community continued with the local nursing committee deciding to engage 3 nurses, two for Eckington and one for Mosborough raising funds from public subscription and local colliery employers.

1921

Domestic and industrial themes dominated at all levels. Coal mining continued to be acrimonious, with Yorkshire news dominated by a legal case between James Walton, MP for Wath on Dearne and the Yorkshire Miners Association. On the local front, J and G Wells announced that they would be giving up Hornthorpe Colliery (see Mining) on the expiry of their lease on 25th March with the loss of 300-400 jobs. This led to the abandonment of a local housing scheme. The poor state of housing continued to be an issue with the Eckington Tenants Protection Society raising several cases of overcharging and outstanding repairs.

Recognisable modern entertainments arrived locally: the Sheffield Premier Jazz Band played at a ball in Eckington and the first advertisement for a picture palace appeared in the paper. Politically, there were local elections in March and in the same month a Women's Labour Party Association was set up in Eckington.

Issues relating to the war are much less common in the paper, and relate mainly to the dedication of further memorials (usually listing the names that appear on them). This was not done for Eckington's, an early one, Marsh Lane's being earlier still.

1922

The major national issue in 1922 was the general election in the autumn of that year. Lloyd George, Prime Minister through the final years of WW1 and after the 1918 General Election had faced increasing opposition from 1921 onwards. At the beginning of 1922, he faced a strong attack from the Duke of Northumberland for misuse of the honours system. The following month a charge of profiteering from the war by selling his memoirs produced an even greater outcry and he was forced to resign. His party, the National Liberals, lost the election, gaining very few seats and Lloyd George himself never held office again. The Conservatives won and the Labour Party, supporting the nationalisation of the mines and railways, a massive house building project and revision of the peace treaties, became the official opposition party. Derbyshire North East (including Eckington) was won by the Labour candidate Frank Lee from Sir Joseph Stanley Holmes (Liberal) with one of the narrowest majorities in history – 15 votes.

Unsurprisingly, after the war ended many towns and villages founded or gave new life to ex-servicemen's clubs. Eckington was no exception. In 1922, the Eckington Ex-Servicemen's Club decided to join with the recently formed, national, British Legion, in order to increase membership and federate with an organisation with common interests. Also under consideration at that time and with a strong likelihood of cross-membership, was a miners' welfare scheme. This would operate as a club and have a headquarters with a reading room, library and hopefully indoor and outdoor games space. The club was formed and headquarters created on Pipeyard Lane, near the Hornthorpe Colliery site.

The Parish Church was upgraded in 1922 with the creation of a new Lady Chapel and altar to the right hand side of the main altar in the 12th Century building. The new chapel was dedicated by the Bishop of Derby. The chapel had a new stained glass window above it, the very beautiful 'Wells Window' memorialising Mary Wells, widow of the late Joseph, who had recently died. Her daughter was the wife of Rector W H Hewson.

There were no more war deaths, but the practice of military funerals was common, especially for high ranking ex-servicemen. Such a funeral was accorded to Co. Sergeant Major Alfred Fanshaw, who had served with the Royal Garrison Artillery, who died in January, aged 51.

1923

New Year greetings were all very domesticated. Reading the papers of the times, it is hard to believe it was less than 5 years since the war ended. Even the resettlement column had now disappeared from the Eckington, Staveley and Woodhouse Express. A new column appeared that year; Motoring and cycling notes. Notes for gardens had replaced the allotments column now that growing vegetables and perhaps having chickens or pigs were less of a necessity.

Motor cycling was very popular. The Eckington Motor Cycle and Light Car Club held a motor cycle test on Bedgreave Hill, Wales, in May. That month also saw the ambulance awards In Eckington. Training in ambulance and first aid skills had started during the war. Nationally, the popular Prime Minister Bonar Law retired and was replaced by Stanley Baldwin.

1924

The start of the New Year was again, not marked by any thundering editorials. Eckington news was only of the Christmas Party and Police Ball. By June, the wedding season was in full flow, with the Eckington wedding of Miss Kathryn Harrison to Mr Ernest Chambers. There were ads for train and bus excursions. Marking the fact that more households now had access to radio, a new column, Broadcasting Notes appeared.

In June there was a report on a new housing scheme planned for Beighton by the Sheffield Coal Company. It was no doubt looked on with envy by the residents of Eckington whose own new housing scheme had been abandoned in 1921.

The 1920s

So the 1920s rolled on, with increasing industrial strife, culminating in the General Strike of 1926. The economy never fully recovered after the War before the years of depression which started with the Wall Street Crash in the USA in 1929 and continued into the 1930s. But at least the years when so many young men died or were maimed seemed to be a thing of the past. They were remembered within families, the community and most particularly on the 11th November each year with solemn ceremony at the War Memorials in Eckington and elsewhere. Sadly, within less than a generation from the end of WW1, Eckington and the rest of Britain and the British Empire was to be at war again with Germany.

Timeline Summary

Year	Key events in Eckington
1914	4th August, UK Government declares War on Germany. Reservist soldiers leave Eckington. Enlistment starts. War continues past Christmas
1915	First deaths and injuries of Eckington military in Gallipoli (Turkey) and France. Enlistment continues. New patterns of life established: cards and letters, home leave, honouring the dead, supporting those serving
1916	1st July, first Battle of the Somme. Huge casualties, Eckington hit hard with deaths and injuries on the day and afterwards
1917	War weariness, heaviest year of death of Eckington men serving. Douglas Henry Wells and Harry Lund die as heroes. Enlistment continues alongside conscription. Hardships at home including food shortages
1918	More optimism. USA enters the War. Heavy fighting, more success including retaking of St Quentin Canal. Hardships at home include 'flu outbreak. 11th November Armistice ends the fighting
1919	Men start return to Eckington to take up previous jobs or seek work. Unemployment high. A small number of deaths continue from wounds and disease. Peace Treaty of Versailles signed on 28th June
1920	Eckington War Memorial dedicated on the 27th June by Mrs Henry Lund in service led by all local church leaders
1921	Hornthorpe Colliery closes
1922	PM Lloyd George and government lose power in second General Election since War. Eckington electorate (including women for second time) elects its first Labour MP, Frank Lee by narrow majority
1923	Life at home becoming more recognisably modern with new interests in gardens, motoring and travel
1924	Households increasingly have access to radio. Family life very important. Little mention of the War in the press

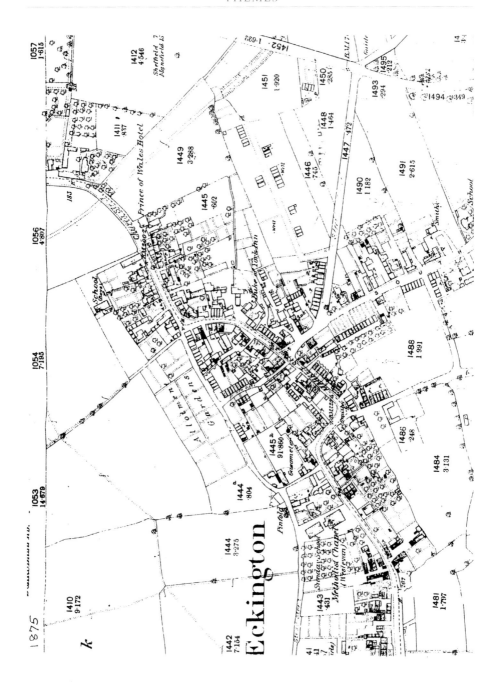

ENLISTMENT

Immediately after the declaration of war, the British Army called up and deployed its Regular Army and called up its Territorials. Eckington Regular army men included J Nightingale and Fred Crouch. Its Territorials included E Nightingale (High Street) and I Nightingale (Dronfield Road), W Redfern and A Staton. There is a very striking story of the first Eckington men leaving the village to go to war days after the declaration of war on 4th August (8th August edition of Eckington, Staveley and Woodhouse Express). 'Enthusiasm at Eckington', recounted that the order calling up the Territorials caused some excitement at Eckington: 'On Tuesday night some of the men assembled at the Cross, a crowd gathered and discussed the war news. It became known that the Territorials would set off

next morning (Wednesday). Early the following morning, Sergeant B Taylor in charge, the men assembled by the Royal Hotel and marched to the Central Railway Station. Some relatives and friends saw them off in touching scenes. The men looked cheerful and fit.'

FAMILY
Will Cartlidge
Informant Mandy Price, Granddaughter

Will Cartlidge
William (Will) Cartlidge had followed his
father Frank into service with the Sitwell
Family. Frank had risen to become head
coachman for the Sitwells. Will remembered
travelling proudly as a boy in 1899, his father
driving the coach taking the Sitwell family
to Cresswell for the laying of the foundation
stone for Saint Mary Magdalene church (by
the 6th Duke of Portland). Ironically years
later, Will returned to Cresswell with his
wife and young family to live in the village.
In his childhood Will lived in an estate
cottage at Renishaw close to what in 1911
was developed as Renishaw Golf Course

by Sir George
Sitwell. The
young Will was a childhood playmate of
Sir George and Lady Ida's children, Edith,
Osbert and Sacheverell. He recalled being
summoned by Lady Ida to account for his
pet rabbit, who had bitten Osbert's finger.
The rabbit did not fare well.

Osbert (later Sir Osbert) was a Guardsman
at the time of the outbreak of WW1 and
was sent to serve in France in the autumn
of that year. Like so many in England, he
had thought the war would be over by
Christmas. As an officer, he tried to make

things as comfortable as possible for his men. He sustained an injury to his arm in France and only served the single term of duty in France. Will was called to service in the Sherwood Rangers Yeomanry, almost certainly at the outbreak of war in 1914, as this was one of the six squadrons of the Royal Yeomanry a light cavalry regiment of the Army Reserve. Before being deployed, the squadron was sent for training at a training camp in Nottinghamshire. The family think that this would be where the young Will met Lois Hastings, from Carlton in Nottingham. The two fell deeply in love and decided to marry before Will was deployed abroad. The marriage was approved by Lois's parents.

Will and his brothers Charles and Colin Cartlidge were all part of the Sherwood Rangers and went to serve together. All three survived the war. Charles returned to his home on Southgate, Eckington with his wife Ada. He lived in the same house until his death at the age of 82. The family lost touch with Colin who also survived the war.

Will's war was a long one and he and Lois had to correspond when he was not home on leave, often using the very beautiful cards that were available to servicemen. Their first of four children was born during the war – the back of one postcard reads 'From your true and ever loving Wife and Baby'.

Finally, after his demobilisation, the family lived on Station Road, Eckington. Will returned to working for the Sitwells. On the day of the birth of his youngest child, his daughter, Lois, he was caddying on the Renishaw golf course. In the early 1920s Sacheverell Sitwell wanted Will to go to the US with him as his batman but Will declined in view of his now substantial family commitments. These were also responsible for his decision to move to Creswell in 1925 to work as a miner to increase his income.

Another man with links to the Sitwell Estate to serve from the beginning of the War was Edmund Bruce Hollingworth, brother to the agent of the Sitwell estate. Bruce Hollingworth was a member of the 9th Battalion of the Sherwood Foresters. The Battalion served in Egypt and Gallipoli in Turkey, where there were heavy losses in 1915, including Eckington men Thomas Farrell and James Oates. Bruce Hollingworth died on the 26th October 1916, a late casualty of the battle of the Somme in July in which the 9th were engaged. Pte Samuel George Smedley was another casualty of the 9th Battalion's deployment in Europe. He died in the first day of the Battle of Thiepval, 26th to 28th September 1916 and Corporal Edwin Simmonds in October 1917. The names of all these early casualties of the war are listed on the Eckington War Memorial. Thomas Farrell's name is also on the Spinkhill Memorial.

Pte Lancelot Ramsden of the King's Own Yorkshire Light Infantry, had parents living at The Cottage, Renishaw Hall, died 28th September 1917 and may have had links to the estate himself. Sergeant B Hambleton who was killed in the same month, had worked for the Sitwell Estate. He was awarded a Military Medal. He was not an Eckington man (his father lived in Bakewell) which probably explains the absence of his name on the Eckington Memorial.

There was pressure to sign up, from colleagues, advertising and local meetings and enlistment fairs. The latter are known to have taken place on the land next to Elmwood, convenient for both Eckington and Mosborough. A local meeting was held at Eckington Assembly Hall on 31st October 1914 chaired by Sir George Sitwell. The hall was packed; there were patriotic songs and a pipe band. Local dignitary Mr J W Turner made a speech concluding with a poem he had composed. The first verse was:

Your country calls! A signal loud and clear
Rings through the land; will you not volunteer
To save your King and home, all you hold dear?

Another speaker was Colonel J C Clayton who had come to Derbyshire from London charged with recruiting

1,000 men. There was a good response at Eckington.

A similar meeting took place early in 1915 at Camms School, Eckington. Rector W R Hewson stressed help was needed to drive the enemy from Belgium and France. There was a need for more men without conscription. "Those who had gone had improved morally and physically" he reportedly said. Private Booth of Mosborough who had gone to the front related some of his experiences. The Chairman remarked that Eckington had done well and furnished about 200 men, as well as any place of its size in Derbyshire. Mr A E Hall (another local dignitary) said men of military age ought to enlist and those not of age ought to be drilling. By this time, locally and nationally there was talk of conscription, although it was a major step and was not in fact introduced until 1916.

Within weeks of the outbreak of war, advertisements had started to appear on hoardings and in newspapers such as these two examples from the Eckington, Staveley and Woodhouse Express.

The 'friends can join together' in one advertisement referred to the Pals regiments where groups could sign up together. These would sometimes be from a single workplace, or location of a club or group such as a football

A Soldier
of the

KING.

AFTER the War every man who has served will command his Country's gratitude. He will be looked up to and *respected* because he answered his country's call.

The Regiments at the Front are covering themselves with Glory.

Field-Marshal Sir John French wrote in an Order of the day,

"It is an Honour to belong to such an Army."

Every fit man from 19 to 38 is eligible for this great honour. Friends can join in a body, and serve together in the same regiment.

Rapid Promotion.

There is rapid promotion for intelligence and zeal. Hundreds who enlisted as private soldiers have already become officers because of their merits and courage, and thousands have reached non-commissioned rank.

Enlist To-day.

At any Post Office you can obtain the address of the nearest Recruiting Office. Enter your name to-day on the Nation's Roll of Honour and do your part.

GOD SAVE THE KING.

1st July 1916 and suffered enormous losses. Eckington did not have such a battalion, and from what is known about the men who died, they joined a very wide spread of regiments and battalions, 22 in all. Even the most common, the Sherwood Foresters (Notts and Derby Regiment) had just over a quarter. They enlisted in quite a variety of places too, Sheffield, Rotherham, Eckington, Killamarsh, Chesterfield. The proximity of Eckington to all these places, and the good links by road and rail would have encouraged this.

On occasions however, men did join up together. Private James Silvers of 18 Northgate, Eckington and his friend Private Arthur Riley who lived on High St, Eckington both joined the 1st Battalion of the Kings own Scottish Borderers. They were 21 and joined up together in January or February 1915. Their numbers are sequential: James was 17503 and Arthur was 17504. James Silvers was killed on 4 June 1915 in the Dardanelles. A memorial service was held for him on Sunday 4 July at Eckington Parish Church – one of the first local lads killed. Arthur Riley was not reported missing until the 17th July, a further letter reporting his death was not received until August, although he had, in fact, died on the same day as his friend James. Later James'

team. Sheffield had a Pals battalion, raised in 1914 and designated as the 12th battalion, York and Lancaster Regiment. Three Eckington men, two with Sheffield connections, served in this battalion. The tragedy of the Pals battalion was that, because of the way that a battalion was deployed if they were unlucky enough to be on the front line when there was active fighting, the losses could be catastrophic. In the case of the Sheffield Pals Battalion, they were deployed as first line on the first day of the Battle of the Somme, younger brother, Reuben Silvers, was also killed (see page 22). Another group of four friends joined the Yorks and Lancaster Regiment; by the end of 1917 only one, F Merrick, was surviving although injured. Friends Harry Bristow, Ernest Hutchinson and Fred Fisher had all died.

Unsurprisingly, given the pressure to enlist and the general atmosphere, younger brothers and young boys generally were often keen to enlist. Sometimes the boys were not even of age – set at 18 from early in the war. There were many examples and it is sometimes hard to believe from the photographic evidence that recruiting officers were fooled. One example of a very young Eckington enlistment was Arnold Morton (pictured right), who enlisted at the age of 16. He survived the War. Another was Arthur Lund (see Lund family).

Some 4.9 million men enlisted in the British Army between 1914 and 1918, 2.4 million before the introduction of conscription in 1916 and 2.5 million afterwards. Of the 2.5 million only an estimated 1.3 million men were actually conscripted (source Professor Ian Beckett, Professor of Military History, University of Kent, 2015). Nevertheless, close to the end of the War, in January 1918, the Government was seeking to conscript more men as it estimated that another

150,000 were needed. The purpose of the Manpower Bill was to allow men in previously reserved occupations such as mining to be called up. There had been concerns that local tribunals, set up to issue exemptions from service, had been doing so fairly freely. There is no evidence that this was the case in Eckington.

THE RETURNERS

This section looks at those who returned from the war. It would be helpful if lists were available, but whilst it is possible to obtain details of medals and individual service, it is not currently possible to obtain lists of all those who served and survived from a particular location. If we work from global statistics (US War Department Report in 1924): approximately 8.9 million British Empire forces were mobilised in WW1, of these 0.9 million (10%) were killed or died (of disease and other causes). 2 million were wounded (22.5%), and almost 200,000 were prisoners or missing (2.2%). This gives a proportion of 35% casualties to service personnel mobilised. Thus about 65% of men who went to war, could be expected to have returned relatively unscathed, although no doubt some with permanent memories which may have amounted to mental health impairment and often with comparatively minor wounds. Over 20% could have returned having sustained more serious wounds. A small percentage (less than 2% when the missing are separated from the prisoners) would have returned after periods as prisoners of war. This gives a total of nearly 90% of service personnel returning.

Using these proportions, if we assume that the 85 men named on the Eckington memorial represent 10% of those who served, then around 850 men were likely to have served from Eckington itself. 439 men appear on the electoral roll for Eckington which was drawn up in the spring of 1918 and included men who were still serving away from home at that time. As the voting age at that time was 21, and many servicemen were between 18 and 20. If we assume that half the men in service in 1918 were under 21 and double the figure on the electoral roll to 878 it comes close to the figure devised by working up from the number killed. This analysis would suggest a figure of 850 or above, as the number of deaths was probably in excess of 85. Hence around 1,000 is probably a reasonable estimate of the number of men from Eckington village who served in WW1.

The returners faced a number of challenges. They had to re-engage with their families, find work, and come to terms with their experiences, and any lasting damage it had caused to their psychological or physical health. In terms of re-engagement with families, we have no direct stories of any difficulties. It is known that these were quite commonly experienced where fathers were re-engaging with children they had hardly seen (or in some cases never seen) for many years. There were also sometimes difficulties with marriages. Whilst the papers report cases of desertion and bigamy, it is easy to imagine the lesser but no less real problems of readjustment after several years of living apart.

With work, some employers re-hired men who had worked for them before enlistment or conscription. Sometimes they had made an undertaking to do this from the start.

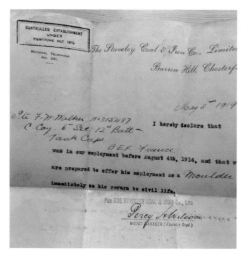

In other cases the work was no longer available or the individual was not able, through injury, to return to it. The period after the war and continuing through the 1920s was not a time of economic prosperity for Great Britain, even before the great global depression of 1929-1933.

The industries of mining and iron foundries nationally and particularly in Eckington were badly affected. Economic historians generally regard Great Britain's recovery in the 1920s to have been somewhat slower than that of France and Germany itself. This is despite the fact that both France and Germany had suffered greater mortality rates than Britain and despite Germany having to pay reparations after the war under the Treaty of Versailles.

In terms of coming to terms with their experiences, there is evidence from ex-servicemen that many did not regret going to war, despite the privations of service, the dangers and the trauma. This is clear in interviews which were given and have been recorded on tape and film from the 1920s onwards to the death of the last veteran, Henry John (Harry) Patch in July 2009. Interviews can be found on the film 'They shall not grow Old', restored for the centenary of the Armistice and shown by the BBC. Many men were, however, very reluctant to speak of what they had witnessed. Sometimes this was life-long. In other cases they became more inclined to talk about their experiences later in life. Locally ex-serviceman Harold Robinson (see page 54) was one of those prepared to talk of his experiences. Some had maintained war diaries which are available. Two local examples are those of Harry Smith and James Godley. Harry Smith, the brother of one of the fallen of Eckington, John Thomas Smith, kept such a diary, now in Eckington Heritage Centre, 6 Southgate, Eckington. Private James Godley, 2nd Battalion, Coldstream Guards, 4th Guards Brigade, the great-grandfather of local historian

Richard Godley, kept a diary covering the Battle of Mons from August 1914 to October 2nd re-produced in the book, 'Renishaw and Spinkhill WW1 and WW2 Project' (2019).

Arranging the demobilisation took quite a time after the signing of the armistice in November 1918. There was also work for the military to do, often inside Germany well into 1919 and even 1920.

FAMILY
Frank William Walker
Informant Ian Marshall, great grandson

Frank William Walker was not demobilised until 1919. As Pte F W Walker he had joined the Tank Corps. His pre-military employment as a shunting driver at the Staveley Iron and Coal works had prepared him well for the Tank Corps. Frank was a keen correspondent, both before and during his war service and many of these letters have survived. He had a correspondence with his friend Adam Starbuck who lived in Eckington. Adam served in the 12th Battn Royal Fusiliers from 1915, so letters from Frank informed him about Eckington life and those from

Adam contained news on mutual friends who had joined up.

After the Armistice Frank spent time in the Cologne area. From the end of WW1 until 1926, Cologne was occupied by the British Army of the Rhine under the terms of the armistice and the subsequent Treaty of Versailles. Frank also visited Berlin before being demobilised in 1919. He collected a number of postcards and photographs of places visited.

He returned to the Staveley Iron and Coal Works which had promised to re-employ him. He became a member of the Ambulance Corps there and also of the Silver Ambulance Brigade in Chesterfield.

Frank was single when he went to war. Keen to settle down, he married Eliza Rose on Christmas Day 1920. They established a household on Handley Road, and had six children. The first, Mary was born in 1921 and was grandmother to informant Ian Marshall.

Another of Ian's great grandparents, Frank Marshall from East Yorkshire, also served in WW1, but was less fortunate than Frank Walker, having been shot in the head and demobilised in consequence in 1918. He married on his return and was self-employed in his own tobacconist's and confectioner's shop in Bridlington. His son James, Ian's grandfather, was born in 1921.

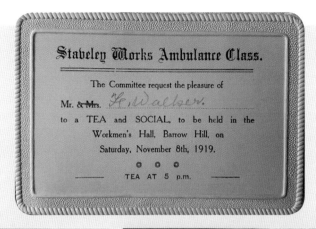

Stabeley Works Ambulance Class.

The Committee request the pleasure of

Mr. & Mrs. *F. Walker.*

to a TEA and SOCIAL, to be held in the
Workmen's Hall, Barrow Hill, on
Saturday, November 8th, 1919.

◎ ◎ ◎

——— TEA AT 5 p.m. ———

F W Walker medals and their original package

Psychological and Physical Health

Sometimes experiences, whilst not talked about, continued to haunt men. Nightmares and night terrors were reported if not by ex-servicemen, then by their wives. Poison Gas (chlorine, phosgene and mustard) was used for the first time in WW1, initially by the Germans, in April 1915, but the Allies followed soon afterwards. It resulted in 1.3 million casualties and 90,000 deaths. Some Eckington men were gassed. Arnold Morton was reported as suffering gas and burns in 1918 for which he was treated in hospital in France. Even more than the numbers who were killed or injured by the gas was the fear it instilled.

Some men were so badly injured that it shortened their lives. Thomas Crouch, father-in-law of Eckington resident Ina Crouch, served in the Cycle Corps. This was a particularly difficult and strenuous role. He used to say he spent more time carrying the cycle than riding it. His health never recovered from his time in service and he died a few years after his return. Frank Marshall, Ian Marshall's great grandfather (see Walker/Marshall family above) died in 1939. In June 1918 the Eckington, Staveley and Woodhouse Express reported that Mr H C Greaves of Market Street had died, having been discharged in

May 1916 and 'ailing for two years' thereafter. He left a widow and three young children. It is likely that many similar deaths into the 1920s and 30s went unreported.

Remarkably, many injured men continued to work and to support families, in some cases singlehanded. Ian Marshall's great-grandfather worked as a tobacconist and confectioner (see above).

Wounded soldiers were cared for in a variety of settings during the war and in the years immediately afterwards. There were military hospitals at home and abroad, looking after patients who remained under military control, and there were over 3,000 temporary auxiliary hospitals provided by the British Red Cross in conjunction with the Order of St John of Jerusalem. These used a variety of buildings from large municipal ones to small private houses across the country. They generally took less seriously injured patients. Staffing was both paid and unpaid. Nursing assistants were often local volunteers. The uniforms were very distinctive; the servicemen wore hospital blues – pale blue jackets and trousers with a red stripe. They could choose whether to wear their regimental caps or non-uniform ones. The nurses wore blue dresses with white aprons with the distinctive Red Cross on the front. The nearest to Eckington seems to have been one at Elmton in Clowne.

FAMILY
Pte Frederick Causier Heptinstall
**Informant Yvonne Anderson,
maternal granddaughter**

A local man, Pte Frederick Causier Heptinstall, Kings Own Yorkshire Light Infantry (KOYLI) was injured in the lower leg, but returned to mining after the war, becoming a mine deputy and sustaining an arm injury in an accident in the Ireland Colliery. After his first wife's early death he brought up their four children single-handed until they left home. He was also an officer in the St John's Ambulance Brigade. During the Second World War he often accompanied local GP Dr Rankin into Sheffield to tend wartime casualties there. On 22nd May 1957 at Buckingham Palace he was presented with the highest award of the Order of St John of Jerusalem. Late in life, his injured leg troubled him more and was amputated. Grandad Hep, as he was known to his family, died in 1965.

FAMILY
Harold Robinson
Informant Olive Newton, Harold's youngest child.

Harold Robinson joined the Cavalry after being called up. He enlisted at Chesterfield, where having expressed a wish to join the cavalry, though not an experienced horseman, his skills were put to the test by a ride round an arena. There was a queue of men waiting their turn to do this. The man before Harold fell (or was thrown) from the horse and was carried away injured. Harold learnt later that the man had died. Following enlistment Harold went on to serve in France and in Egypt. He had a natural aptitude for horses and always said that he loved them.

He often spoke about his wartime experiences, especially in Egypt where he was struck both by the geographical and cultural differences of the local men, who served alongside the British servicemen. Camels (dromedaries) were used alongside horses there. The weather was hot and dry and Harold had a distinct memory of the local men stopping their activities on a march and kneeling in prayer. The cause turned out to be the appearance of a raincloud. On duty one night he was stabbed by a local man, and had to return home injured. He was quite disabled at this point and was stretchered onto a ship for the long journey home. The ship, the HMS Teutonic, was a White Star Line Steamship being used as a troop carrier. Harold retained a photograph of the ship throughout his life. He had several souvenirs when he left port, stored in his boots including the knife with which he had been stabbed. These were lost on the homeward journey.

It is not entirely clear what happened to Harold on his discharge save that he returned to Eckington. There is a picture of a group of men and a nurse which was found locally (see below). All are in hospital blues and the nurse is wearing a Red Cross uniform. The man in the picture in the civilian cap bears considerable resemblance to Harold Robinson. No other personnel in the photos have been identified. There is also uncertainty about the building. At one point it seemed possible it was Eckington Drill Hall. This building stood on Littlemoor until 2017 when it was demolished to make way for an Aldi store. It is well remembered as a dance venue for many decades. Quite when it was built is unclear but it seems most likely to have been the late 1920s or early 1930s.

Soon after his return and recovery Harold Robinson became engaged and married a local woman, Nellie Deffley, whose family lived on Pipworth Lane where they had a milk round, which Harold helped run after their marriage. They established a home on Bole Hill and started a family. Sadly, Nellie died when their two children Eileen and Victor were aged 11 and 9. It was another low point in Harold's life as he lost both Nellie and his parents within 3 years. He advertised for a carer and May French, applied and started to work as a live in housekeeper. May was from the Eckington Newsagent family who had two shops at that time,

the 'upper' shop at 9 West Street and the bottom shop in the town centre. To avoid gossip, Harold suggested to May that they marry. May agreed, despite the 18 year age difference. They went on to have two children of their own, Kenneth and Olive, living first at John Street and then Henry Street in Eckington. During this marriage Harold worked shifts as a furnace man at Renishaw Iron works. He died at the age of 91. He is buried in Eckington Cemetery, first joining Nellie, later to be joined by May.

Prisoners of War

The Allies and the Germans took prisoners throughout WW1. It is estimated that by the end of the war 2.4 million prisoners were being held by Germany, mainly in approximately 300 camps on German soil. The Hague Convention which governed the conduct of Nations in regard to prisoners of war had been signed by Western Nations (including Germany, France, Britain and Russia) in 1907. They covered aspects of life in prison, including lodging, work, religion, food dress and mail. These conditions were not fully observed, at least partly because of the pressure that the numbers placed on the Germany captors. There was illness in the camps because of the poor condition of the accommodation and poor and inadequate food left prisoners hungry and more vulnerable to illness. Typhus, Cholera and lung diseases were common. There were deaths among prisoners from these and other causes. Some prisoners would have been injured in combat before capture. Red Cross parcels helped ameliorate this by supplementing the food. Mail, whilst subject to censorship and sometimes denied, did get through. The Hague Conventions gave each prisoner a right to write two letters and 4 postcards. Officers were generally treated better, in terms of their conditions.

Thirty-two WW1 prisoners with links to Eckington were found through a search on www.findmypast.co.uk. Some of these were verified through coverage in the Eckington, Staveley and Woodhouse Express and other sources. Other prisoners, including Pte T Hutton and John Smith, not on the list below were recorded by the paper as released in early 1919.

First Name	Surname	Date of Birth	Date of Capture	Notes
Sidney	Adlington	1891		
James T	Barber	1880		
James Thomas	Barker	1889	21/03/1918	Died 20/7/1918. Married, lived on Fanshawe Road, Eckington. On Memorial
Thomas	Barsvy			
Frank	Broomfield	1880		
Herbert	Clayton	1895		
Hubert	Cummins	1892		
Wilfred	Davison	1896		
Fred	Dinsdale	1891		
Frank	Evans	1894		
Jack	Fenton			
Albert	Grayson			
William	Green	1887	1918	Bombardier, married, Market Street
Leonard	Guy	1897		
Arnest E	Harding	1898		
John	Hipwell	1892		
Andrew	Hopkinson			
Albert Edward	Jones			Confirmed. A.E Jones , MM
Frank	Kirby		21/3/1918	Confirmed. Lance Corporal F Kirby, youngest son of Mr & Mrs A C Kirby, Northgate, Eckington.
Thomas A	Knowles			

William	Littlewood				
Alfred	Marriott	1881			
Isaac	Middleton	1884			
Frank	Midwinter	1893			
George James	Osborne	1886			
Edwin	Price	1893			
Albert	Rhodes				
Frank	Riley	14/03/1896	21/03/1918 Bullecourt	2/6 Notts & Derbys 241678	
William	Robinson	24/01/1898	28/03/1918 Gommecourt	Pte, 5th KOYLI, 205593	
Arthur E	Tudor	1892			
Francis	Verden				

The case of Albert Edward Jones is a happy one. Missing, thought dead, his postcard from captivity not only confirmed his survival but also that he had been awarded the Military Medal prior to capture (see Medals). There was a much less happy outcome for James T Barker, who died after four months imprisonment.

Bombardier R R Green was one of the first prisoners of war to return after the armistice in November 1918. He had served 7-8 months in Belgium and complained of harsh treatment, including that meted out towards women and children civilians. As was the case with a number of prisoners of war, especially towards the end of the war, he was expected to work in farming. In one communication home, he said he had been grooming horses. The prisoner of war experience of Capt Norman L Wells, grandson of George Wells, of the J and G Wells mining company is related later in the Wells family story. As an officer, Capt Wells would expect better treatment than other ranks but his treatment was very harsh.

COMMEMORATION
Memorials

The memorials abroad, close to where men had fallen are described and pictured in the WW1: Eckington Soldiers and their Families booklet commemorating the centenary of the Armistice. The major ones containing the names of many local men who were killed, include the memorials at Thiepval on the site of the Somme battlefield in France, Tyne Cot in Belgium, Menin Gate at Ypres, Arras in France and Helles in modern Turkey marking the Gallipoli conflict. All these monuments were established during the 1920s by the Commonwealth War Graves commission through which they have been impeccably maintained since. Relatives and others started to visit the graves and memorials of their loved ones in the 1920s, always supposing that they knew where the grave or memorial was.

Will Cartlidge's wife, Lois Hastings, lost her brother, Alfred Hastings, MM, in the War. Her mother was so distraught having received the telegram informing her of his death that his name was never mentioned again and her daughter was unaware of what happened to him. Granddaughter Mandy subsequently discovered through the Commonwealth War Graves Commission that Lance

Corporal Alfred Hastings 32253 A Company, 5th Battalion of the Sherwood Foresters (Notts and Derby Regiment) had died on 11th April 1918 aged 21 and was buried in the Neiderwehen Cemetery in Kassel, Germany. Sadly her grandmother had died before Mandy was able to tell her. The family have since visited the grave.

In the UK national memorials including the London Cenotaph (officially opened on 11 November 1920) were erected and the Unknown Soldier was interred on the same day in nearby Westminster Abbey, simultaneously with one in France. The USA WW1 memorial and tomb of their WW1 Unknown Soldier was established in 1921 at the Arlington National Cemetery. The military had their own memorials including the Sherwood Foresters Memorial at Crich, near Matlock, which contains the names of the fallen who served with the regiment (https:historicengland.org. uk/listing/the-list/list-entry/1072594). Locally monuments were established in all the local villages, and in many churches, schools and workplaces. In January 1918 at the suggestion of Mr T Butler, Chair of the Eckington Parish Council, a recognition committee was established to consider how best to remember those who had served their country in the military and naval services, in particular those who had made the supreme sacrifice (they knew of 116 deaths at this point) and those who

The Great Sacrifice.

To the Memory of
Private Albert Edris Moody. K.O.Y.L.I.
killed in Action in France.
Sep. 14th 1918
From the Eckington War Recognition Committee.
Chairman.

had received medals. They decided on an immediate letter of appreciation to the bereaved. A month later the Eckington and District War Relief Fund decided on a £2 payment (£104 at 2020 values) to each of the bereaved families. Later, yet another local committee, with Mr T Greensmith and Mr W Sewell (manager for J and G Wells) as President and vice president, was making arrangements for each bereaved family to receive a copy of the picture entitled 'The Great Sacrifice'. This picture, very well-known during WW1 was by James Clark. Each one given was signed by Mr Greensmith.

Collecting money towards the parish monument/s started at this point. The receipts of a flag day were reported to the recognition committee in May by individual village: Eckington, Ridgeway, Marsh Lane, Mosborough and Halfway. Later, after the armistice, the recognition committee, having already decided on a monument near the church discussed whether there should be anything further. Various suggestions including a hospital, alms-houses, or a health visitor were discussed. The eventual decision was to apply for two captured German guns. Two guns were purchased but there was a subsequent debate between the Parish Council and Sir Osbert Sitwell, who was concerned that the guns should promote peace but feared they may not. One, a German Howitzer, was briefly displayed at the Renishaw end of Southgate before both were sold.

A plan of the proposed Eckington War Memorial was approved in December 1918. The plan was supplied by G Maile and Son, 367 Euston Road, London, specialising in church sculpture at that time. The design was for a grey Cornish granite pillar with a Celtic cross, 16 feet high, including plinths with names of the fallen inscribed. The location was to be on the green close to the church, rising above Church Street.

There were thoughts of a single memorial for the Civic Parish of Eckington, but each ward wished to have their own. This was not an uncommon view: Derbyshire has a total of 3,500 memorials of all types (https:www.derbyshirewarmemorials. com). The decision led to localised fund raising. Halfway installed a small cardboard cross in the wooden Methodist Chapel on New Street Halfway to encourage local giving. The permanent, beautifully carved memorial was dedicated in 1922.

Marsh Lane's was dedicated in August 1919 (26 names). Renishaw, Spinkhill Ridgeway, Killamarsh and Barlborough are other local Derbyshire ones. Mosborough and Halfway are now in Sheffield, together with other local ones in Gleadless, and Intake. Eckington's was erected and dedicated in June 1920. Quite an early one; it was reported in the Eckington, Staveley and Woodhouse Express. There were later dedications across the NE Derbyshire/South Yorkshire area that the newspaper covered.

MEDALS
Campaign Medals

Many local men were awarded campaign medals, the 1914 Star or 1914-15 Star, the British War Medal and the Allied Victory Medal. These three medals were sometimes irreverently referred to as Pip (Star), Squeak (War Medal) and Wilfred (Victory Medal) after Daily Mirror cartoon characters well known at the time.

The Star (Pip) was an award for service from the earliest part of the war (2.4 million issued). The Stars would have been quite common in Eckington and the surrounding area as many men enlisted early in the War. The 1914 Star, sometimes referred to as the Mons Star (for service in the theatre of war between 5th August 1914 and 22/23rd November that year) is less common than the 1914-1915 Star (only 365,622 were issued) but some Eckington men would have been eligible. They have a clasp (bar) with the dates.

Much less common even than the Mons Star is the Territorial Force War Medal, 1914-1919. Those eligible had to belong to the Territorial Force or Territorial Force Nursing Service to be eligible. They had to have been a member of the Territorial Force before 30th September 1914 and to have served in an operational theatre of war outside the UK at some time during WW1. An estimated 34,000 were issued. Holders having this medal would not have a 1914 or 1914-5 Star. Some of the Eckington men were Territorials and would have been eligible.

The War Medal (Silver), known as the 'Squeak', was for service in a theatre of war or abroad at any time during the war (6.5 million issued). The Victory Medal (Gilt), the' Wilfred', was awarded to all those holding a Territorial, a Star 1914 or a 1914-1915 Star and most of those who were eligible for a War Medal were also eligible for the Victory Medal (5.7 million issued). The British War Medal and Victory Medal pair on display together is sometimes known as Mutt and Jeff. For both these two medals, the recipient's service number, rank, name and unit were impressed on the rim.

The Silver War Badge (sometimes referred to as the Silver Wounds Badge or Kings Badge), was most usually given to those who were discharged or retired from the military forces as a result of sickness or injury caused by their war service. This was later (1918) extended to include those civilians who had served with the Royal Army Medical Corps, female nurses, staff and aid workers. An estimated 1,150,000 were issued. They had an accompanying certificate but not an engraved name. The award helped those who had been discharged to dispel any suggestion that they were avoiding service. 'White feathering', criticising those 'not in khaki' was common in all communities in WW1. A particularly sad local case reported in the Eckington, Staveley and Woodhouse Express was that of a master butcher, rejected for service because he was 'down' (depressed), who committed suicide after such taunting.

Nationally, the next of kin of those killed received a large bronze plaque, the size of a small tea plate, which became popularly known as the 'death penny'.

Far left:
Star and Bar

Above:
Pip, Squeak and Wilfred

Left:
Territorial Force Medal

Above: Silver War Badge and Certificate

Right: Death Penny

Bravery Awards

There were a number of men from Eckington who won medals for bravery during the WW1. The Military Medal (established in March 1916) was awarded to personnel of the British Army below commissioned rank for bravery in battles on land. The Military Cross was awarded for act/s of exemplary gallantry during active operations to captains or officers of lower rank. Two of the families (Harry Lund, Douglas Henry Wells with a Military Medal or Military Cross respectively are included in the family portraits). Sadly, both of these men were killed.

Others from Eckington itself who are known to have won the Military Medal and who survived are (in date order):

Sergeant Sidney Harrison, 13396 Leicesters, and listed as from

Eckington in the award list of the London Gazette (cutting courtesy of David Nightingale). The Eckington, Staveley and Woodhouse Express also reported this honour, giving his parents' address as 25 Pinfold Street. His brother, Private William Harrison had made the ultimate sacrifice, dying on 9th June, 1916. He is memorialised on the Eckington memorial and in France where both brothers served.

Harold Wilson Ward, son of George Ward, 50 Chesterfield Road, Eckington. He was the first Eckington man to win a Military Medal, according to Derbyshire Times of 4th September 1916. He was a land valuation officer at Chesterfield prior to his war service.

Sergeant Samuel Argyle, was awarded his Military Medal late in 1916. It was reported in the Eckington, Staveley and Woodhouse Express on 23rd December of that year. Sergeant Argyle had moved to Nottingham on his marriage, but his mother still lived on Southgate. He would have been well known as he had been a member of the Eckington Prize Band. He was an ambulance man in the war and was awarded his medal for bringing in the wounded in circumstances where he was the only survivor from a team of 8.

Corporal Albert Edward Jones, Sherwood Foresters, son of Mr and Mrs Jones of Hornthorpe Road, Eckington was awarded a Military Medal in 1917. The citation referred to his 'great courage and coolness'. He had subsequently been taken prisoner and held in Germany between the 21st and the 23rd March 1918. He reported the Military Medal in a card sent to his home. His family must have been delighted by the news, not so much of the medal but to know he was alive. Prior to his letter he had been reported missing, thought to have been killed in action. A memorial service was held for him in the Wesleyan Chapel at the end of April, a combined service also for Albert T Rhodes but whilst the latter had died (and is buried in Eckington church yard and has his name on the Eckington memorial),

the service fortunately proved to have been premature in the case of Albert Edward Jones.

Duncan Crawford, one of the 7 sons of Mrs Crawford of 85 Market Street serving in WW1, had been awarded a Military Medal for bravery whilst serving in France in 1917.

Gunner William Levick (second son of Joseph Levick of Market Street) was awarded a MM in December 1917. Aged 40, a miner at Hartington Colliery, he had enlisted in October 1915, going on to serve in France and be awarded his MM for gallantry and devotion to duty on the battlefield.

Private Albert Adams, second son of Mr and Mrs Adams of Staveley Road, was awarded the Military Medal for conspicuous bravery in the field reported the Eckington, Staveley and Woodhouse Express on 27th July 1918.

Pte Ernest Fells, an Eckington man, latterly living in Hackenthorpe.

Sergeant Sam Hadfield (pictured), Sherwood Foresters, of Sitwell Street, Eckington.

The last two were reported in the Eckington, Staveley and Woodhouse Express in early 1919.

This is likely to be an underestimation. In addition there were awards to people in other parts of the Civic Parish of Eckington, for example Sgt Frank Bond of the Toronto Regiment in Canada, who emigrated to Canada having worked as a miner for J and G Wells. He was killed in action in May 1917 and posthumously awarded the Military Medal. He is commemorated on the Renishaw church memorial.

The highest bravery award won locally as far as is known was the Victoria Cross awarded to Corporal Fred Greaves of Barlborough. Corporal (later Sergeant) Greaves served in the 9th Battalion of the Sherwood Foresters (23715). He was awarded the VC for 'most conspicuous bravery, initiative and leadership' in fighting East of Ypres in Belgium on 4th October 1917 when his platoon came under machine gun fire. Fred Greaves lived to return from the war and thereafter this self-effacing and popular man took part in many commemorations. There are three men with the name Greaves on the Eckington memorial. They are possibly part of the extended Greaves family.

FAMILY
Harry Lund
Audio. Informant Debbie Hyde, great niece of Harry

Harry Lund was an Eckington man living at 8 School Street at the time of the outbreak of war in 1914. Aged 28, he was married to Mary Elizabeth (Lizzie) with a very young family. He was a plumber, working for the local gas company. An ardent supporter of Sheffield Wednesday, he carried a little silver owl matchbox with him at all times and attended all home matches at Hillsborough, catching a special direct bus from Eckington.

In January 1915, he enlisted voluntarily with the 11th Brigade Royal Field Artillery and was despatched to serve in France after training. His employers said that he could not expect a job on his return. He served until the end of 1917 when he was seriously wounded in France and died the same day, 28th December, after an act of bravery for which he was awarded the Military Medal.

During the time he served there was a regular exchange of letters and photos with home. In one letter with a photograph, he asked Lizzie whether his son Edgar recognised him. On one period of leave he came across his

much younger brother, Arthur then 16 standing on the corner of School Street, unwilling to go home. When pushed to explain himself, Arthur said he had enlisted and been accepted for service in the Sherwood Foresters. Harry gave him a clip round the ear and told him to go home. On his last period of leave Harry was particularly upset to return to the front as he felt he would not survive to see his family again. He had to be almost pushed onto the train. He was correct in his anticipation. Younger brother Arthur survived the War. When Harry died Arthur was serving in the trenches and received the news 'down the line'. He said it hadn't really registered; there were so many deaths at the time.

At home, Lizzie was distraught. She and Harry had two children by this time, Edgar and his younger sister, Bessie. They received news that Harry was seriously wounded and the following day that he had died. He had received the Military Medal for his bravery in the action in which he was killed. Detailed reports appeared in the  local press in January 1918. They reported that the letter from Harry's commanding officer on the 29th December had said:

'I am very sorry to tell you that your husband, Sergeant Lund, was wounded rather badly yesterday, 28th December 1917. We have every hope of him pulling through. I cannot tell you anymore. You will be pleased he has gained the Military Medal. I hope you will have good news of him soon. The Battery will miss him very much.'

Sadly, there was no better news: the following week the paper reported the death of the Sergeant Lund on his way to the field ambulance. It said that 'the gallant officer (sic) had received the Military Medal for taking up ammunition and bringing back wounded under heavy fire.'

Months later, there was an article describing how Edgar, then 6 years had received his father's medal in a service at Endcliffe Hall, Sheffield. A family story told how his widow Lizzie had thrown the medal on to the open fire. It was snatched off again by her mother-in-law. Lizzie never re-married. The family remained in School Street. Bessie was educated with the help of financial support from Henry Lund, Harry's uncle, a successful painter and decorator who owned houses for rent in Sheffield and Eckington. Bessie Lund went on to become head-teacher at Camms School, Eckington, a stones-throw from her lifelong home (8 School Street) which she latterly shared

with Dorothy Booth. Edgar joined the family painting and decorating business and went on to serve in WW2. In what must have been a heart-stopping moment for the family, he was missing at one point but fortunately resurfaced and survived.

A third brother, William Charles, known as Charlie, also served in WW1 as a Lewis gunner. Charlie visited his brother's grave after the war. Henry Lund gave both of his surviving nephews £100 on their return from WW1. Arthur went to work as a painter and decorator with Eyres. The youngest of the brothers, Harold went on to work in the family business when of an age to do so. Henry supported his orphaned great nephew and niece. He also made a significant contribution to the Eckington Memorial Fund. Probably on account of these actions,

Mr. Woodhead, Miss Lund, Mr. Wilde, Mrs. Moore, Mr. Kennon
Mrs. Hodkin, Miss Harness, Mrs. Taylor, Miss Edwerds

Harry's heroism and his involvement with the church during his life (he was a regular communicant and Sunday School teacher), Henry's wife unveiled the monument on 27th June 1920.

Harry's brother Arthur was courting by the end of the War and, once demobbed, married Harriet Ellen Glasby and established his own family,

daughter Muriel and son Harry, named after his late brother. Arthur had come across the French name Muriel in a book he read when he was serving in France. Life became no easier at the end of the war or beyond. Harriet spent much time serving the community:

during the war she had sung to injured troops in Sheffield, 'Where have all the Flowers gone?' being a particular favourite. In 1918 and 1919, influenza affected many people in Eckington and, although not a professional nurse, she nursed several members of the local community, fortunately without becoming ill herself. Life continued hard through the 1920s. Muriel remembered as a child in 1929 one of her grandmothers taking a turnip from a local field; an act of some desperation. Arthur commented on the famous Lloyd George pledge to create a 'Land fit for Heroes' that you had to be a hero to live in the land!

Regimental Remembrance: Sherwood Foresters

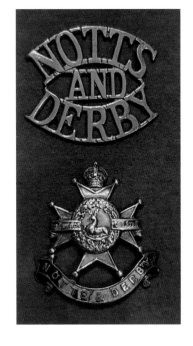

Regiments proudly remember the sacrifices of their WW1 men, over more than a century since the end of the War and despite many amalgamations and changes to the UK's defence forces. The Sherwood Foresters is now part of the Mercia Regiment. Its annual pilgrimage on the first Sunday in July each year at Crich first took place in 1923, when the remodelled memorial tower was completed. Originally attended by families and ex-service men who had served alongside their fallen colleagues, it is now more likely to be attended by their grandchildren or greatgrandchildren.

FAMILY
William Redfern
Informant John Redfern, grandson.

William 'Staffy' Redfern was born on 10 March 1889 in Staffordshire. He came to North Derbyshire when his father died from pneumonia working in the infamous Hailstone Quarry in Staffordshire. He joined the Sherwood Foresters as a Territorial in 1907 and was called for active service abroad very early in the War. He served with the 1st/6th Battalion (Reg. No. 2254) until he returned home after being bayonetted very badly while rescuing his brother Arthur who had been captured by the Germans. After his recovery he served briefly in the 'Black & Tans' in Ireland at the time of the 1916 uprising, but then returned to France in 1917 and joined the 1st/5th Battalion for a while (Reg. No. 240491) before re-joining the 1st/6th where he served out his time until the close of war and finally stood down on 24 Jan 1919.

The family did not escape loss in WW1. John Redfern's maternal grandmother lost her brother James Alfred Herring, an Eckington man serving with the 10th Battalion of the Yorks and Lancs Regiment, who was killed in action in 1917.

William Redfern was latterly a Company Sergeant Major in The Notts & Derbys Regiment (The Sherwood Foresters) and was awarded the British War Medal, the 1915 (Mons) Star, and the Victory Medal. The Pip, Squeak, and Wilfred as described above. Other long service medals were awarded later along with some for service in WW2.

He continued to serve in the Territorials after 1919, working latterly in mining rather

than market gardening which had been his first calling. At the outbreak of WW2 he returned to active service but was invalided out in 1941 after two years of service in WW2. After that he organised diversionary lights in the Moss valley to try to divert German Bomber Raids from populated areas. He served the Regiment for a total of 34 years in all. He died in 1958 when living at Mill Road, Eckington. 3 Regimental Colonels of the Sherwood Foresters and many men of other ranks attended his funeral.

Mercia Regiment's Family Day

Poppy Day

Remembrance Day, the anniversary of the Armistice on the 11th November each year was immediately adopted from 1919 onwards, replacing the marking of each anniversary of the marking of Britain's declaration of war on 4th August. The first Poppy appeal took place in 1921 when the poppy was a representation on a postcard. The poppy was and remains a potent reminder of the fallen as they grew in abundance in Flanders fields where so many men were killed and wounded in WW1.

The first appeal by Earl Haig in support of ex-servicemen was very successful. The British Legion, established by Earl Haig to care for ex-servicemen and their dependents, took on responsibility for fund-raising through an annual poppy appeal. Factories manned by disabled ex-servicemen were set up to produce the poppies. Volunteers were involved in selling the poppies on behalf of the British Legion. Focusing the wearing of poppies on Remembrance Day and using the poppies in wreaths was strongly established from the early 1920s. The sea of poppies around the Tower of London to mark the centenary of the end of WW1 in 2018 was particularly memorable.

HOME FRONT
Industry

This section provides a background to the occupations of the men who went to serve in the war from Eckington and the surrounding area. The principal local sources of employment were mining, iron foundry and metal trades and farming.

When conscription was introduced in January 1916 under the Military Service Act mining became a reserved occupation along with munitions work. Iron foundry and agriculture were partially excluded. The Act initially made medically fit single men aged 19 to 41 eligible for conscription unless they were in a reserved occupation. In May the Military Service Act Number 2 extended this to married men, lowered the age limit to 18 and increased the upper age limit to 50. It was possible to appeal, and request total, conditional or temporary exemptions. The local tribunal was established by the Chesterfield Rural District Council in December 1915, and held its first meeting in January 1916 and its last in October 1918. In this time it dealt with 5,000 cases across the area it served, meeting almost weekly. Most cases approved were for temporary exemption. An agricultural officer usually sat with the tribunal. Numbers from Eckington were relatively low, probably on account of the unambiguously excluded position of mining. However, a large number of miners enlisted voluntarily both before the introduction of conscription and afterwards.

Mining

Mining was the most significant industry in and around Eckington through the 19th and 20th Centuries. By the time of WW1, it had begun a long period of decline towards the 1980s when the last pit closed (other than some very small scale workings which still continue). Such was its significance that for a long time an Eckington without mining would have been impossible to contemplate.

In June 1963 the National Union of Mineworkers (NUM) erected a commemorative plaque in the George Inn at Eckington to mark and celebrate the foundation of the Miners Association which was a forerunner of the NUM. In 1987 Renishaw Park Colliery closed in acrimonious circumstances, as was so often the case in the industry.

Some of the main collieries operating in and around Eckington at the time of WW1 were:

Renishaw Park Colliery

Situated on the Staveley-Eckington Road close to Eckington and adjoining the Sitwell estate, Renishaw, it is believed that the shafts were sunk in 1860 and the Thirbycliffe shaft in 1868. J and G Wells were mining the Flockton Seam in 1914 at Thirbycliffe and Renishaw Park under an agreement with Sir George Sitwell, the landowner. In this year water from the nearby River Rother flooded the pit and caused its abandonment. Sir George went on to win considerable compensation from J and G Wells. Renishaw was not re-opened until 1929, after Mr Reg Horrocks, a mining engineer had successfully dealt with the water problems which took him several years (The Coal Mining Industry of Sheffield and North Derbyshire, Ken Wain 2014). Furnace Hill Colliery was another colliery operational in the

1920s and managed by R E Horrocks. Mr Horrocks is the man in the bowler hat on the left in the picture.

This colliery was closed on the re-opening of Renishaw Park in 1929. From the point of view of WW1 history, the closure of Renishaw Park probably contributed to unemployment in the industry through the war years and the 1920s. It may well have added to the temptation to enlist in the military.

Hornthorpe Colliery

This colliery was quite close to Renishaw Park, even more central to Eckington, although not as surrounded by housing as the former site is today. It was closer to the West Street.

Like Renishaw Park, it was leased to J and G Wells at the time of WW1

by Sir George Sitwell. Also in common with Renishaw Park it was difficult to keep in a dry condition – constant pumping was necessary. In 1921 this colliery was closed on the expiry of the lease. The men were redeployed into other J and G Wells collieries. The closure of Hornthorpe meant that, taken together with Renishaw Park the case for new houses was harder to make for Eckington, in contrast with Killamarsh.

Holbrook Colliery

This colliery was at Halfway, towards Killamarsh. It was well within walking distance for miners from Eckington, Mosborough and Killamarsh as well as the village of Halfway itself. It was a large employer of miners at the time of WW1. There was a related colliery at Norwood, further towards Killamarsh, and sometimes known as Holbrook No. 2. Again both were owned by J and G Wells Ltd., along with Westthorpe Colliery, Killamarsh where the first shaft was sunk in 1923. Westthorpe thrived in the 1920s and additional houses were built for workers in Killamarsh.

Hornthorpe and Holbrook were the largest local collieries at the time of WW1 although there were many other smaller mines of varying sizes and types. The owners of Hornthorpe and Holbrook, J and G Wells Ltd., together with other major colliery owners, won a tribute from the Derbyshire Miners Association in August 1914 for providing allowances for food and rent for families with breadwinners away at the war. Later, the company provided money to those families who had lost a breadwinner: in February of 1918, the company gave £5 (worth just under £300 at 2020 prices) to each widow or mother of fallen ex-employees.

Mining work was hard, physically dangerous, with poor working conditions, prone to industrial disputes, and with lower pay than in the services. From the point of view of the services, miners were fit and had many useful skills. In the early years of WW1, 1914 and 1915, enlisting must have seemed a better option. There was also a strong sense of comradeship within the industry. There was tremendous pressure for voluntary enlistment as shown in the section above in the twenty months between outbreak of war and the introduction of conscription.

Many hundreds, if not into the thousands of Eckington and district miners served in the military in WW1. Many paid the ultimate sacrifice: in all it is estimated that over 3,000 miners from North East Derbyshire gave their lives in WW1.

FAMILY
Douglas Wells
Informants John Redfern, Kath Murphy and Philip Staton.

There is no informant for the Wells family story. However, such is their significance to the local scene around the time of the WW1, as major colliery owners and in having one of the two Military Cross/ Medal awards held by those who are commemorated on the Eckington Memorial, Douglas Henry Wells, that it seemed appropriate to cover his family story.

Douglas Henry Wells was born in Eckington in 1892, he was the grandson of George Wells, the 'G' of the J and G Wells and Co. mining company, the J being his great uncle Joseph Wells. The men of the family had relatively short lives, some falling prey to pit accidents in their own mines. George Wells lived on Southgate, in the large house then known as Hohenlinden, later as Southgate House and more recently The Grange. He died in 1871, with his colliery interests being taken over by his son George Henry Wells, third eldest of his 13 children. George Henry also died comparatively young; born in 1852, he died in 1905, leaving a young family. His wife Isabella Lewis Costin predeceased him in 1899, leaving five children as wealthy orphans.

Douglas Henry and his elder brother Norman Lewis Wells left Eckington after their father's death as young boys. They lived in Canada with relatives until the outbreak of WW1 when, now in their twenties they returned and enlisted in British regiments. Douglas Henry enlisted in the Yorks and Lancs Regiment, 5th Battalion. As 2nd Lieutenant, he was killed in action in France, on 3rd May 1917, awarded a Military Cross for his bravery. He is remembered on the Arras memorial, near to where he fell, on the

gravestone of his parents in Eckington cemetery and in the Canadian book of remembrance, where the page bearing his name is displayed annually.

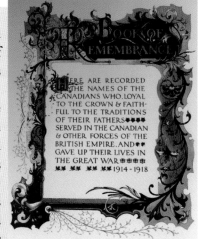

Douglas Henry's Eckington links were significant and he was remembered in a memorial service held in the Eckington Wesleyan Church (or Chapel; the titles seem to have been used interchangeably) of which his parents had been members and leaders. The Wells family is believed to have provided the original funding to found the Church. Two other recent casualties were remembered at the same time, Major Frederick Vickers, of the 15th Battalion Sherwood Foresters and Leonard Butler, a sergeant with the Royal Field Artillery. The Wesleyan Church had suffered seven casualties by this time.

Norman Wells was a prisoner of war at the time of his brother's death. His account of his treatment and his views on Germany

were carried in September 1918, in a full page newspaper article, under a heading of

'Tunnelling to Escape; Eckington Officer's Gross Treatment in Germany; How Prisoners were betrayed'

It is a first person account by Capt Norman L Wells, of Eckington, of his treatment as a prisoner of war. He describes transfer to prison camp in poor conditions without comfort or food and drink, even for the lame and ill; strip searches on arrival and housing next door to the pig-sties. The prisoners had an allocation of 2 blankets each. Ferocious dogs were used inside the wire boundary fence each night. An attempt to tunnel out was foiled. Capt Wells was ultimately released. He concludes that it is 'impossible to talk of peace with Germany' given their treatment of prisoners. Whilst Capt Wells would not have been an objective observer there was certainly a lot of prisoner taking towards the end of the war and conditions are likely to have been much as he described. Norman Wells survived the war and went on to marry Helen Mary McCabe and establish a family. He did not return to live in Eckington. He died in 1965.

The last member of the Wells family to live in the area was Helen Margaret Jane Wells, born in 1891. She was the daughter of Sophia Wells, and granddaughter of Joseph Wells and Mary Habershon. Sophia had married her cousin William Edwin Wells on 11th August 1881 at the Parish Church of St Peter  and Paul in Eckington. He was the son of George Wells and an uncle of Douglas and Norman Wells. Joseph Wells had built the spectacular Eckington Hall as his family home which was completed in 1871, only two years before his death. Sophia had moved from Eckington into the Hall on its completion.

By the time of his death, Joseph had also commenced work on the neighbouring Elmwood House. Edwin completed the work and it became his family home. Widowed early, Sophia continued to live there bringing up their three children. At her death in 1935, Elmwood was left to her daughter Helen Margaret Jane Wells. A kind and generous

lady, Miss Wells, a spinster, continued to live in the house until her death in 1977. It is often said that there was a dearth of marriageable men as a consequence of WW1. Whilst such a gap was not as great as myth would have it, it is partially true particularly in the officer group where the deaths were proportionately greater. It is possible that Miss Wells lost a fiancé in the WW1 and there is a local story to that effect but other than to note that she was of marriageable age at that time (23 at the outbreak of war), it is not possible to verify this.

Mining was a troubled industry from the beginning of the 20th Century. There were frequent disputes over pay and conditions and strikes and national consideration of how to improve the industry. Strikes continued through WW1: there was a particularly long running strike of the Yorkshire Miners only settled in August 1918. Only a month later and possibly related to the strike, there was still unrest with the Yorkshire Miners Association fighting for 25 men who had been victimised or dismissed.

Nationalisation of the industry began to be discussed as a possible solution but was not always popular. The Eckington, Staveley and Woodhouse Express which covered a number of mining areas wrote in an editorial '... and we need not assume that State Ownership or Nationalisation will be a panacea for trade disputes'. It was, nevertheless, the recommendation of the Coal Commission in the Sankey Report of June 1919. It was to take another war and almost another twenty years before it happened.

Ironworks

The second major industrial occupation for Eckington men was ironwork. Renishaw Foundry was probably one of the largest foundries in Britain during the 19th Century. However, the firm had started to decline by the early years of the 20th Century. It was operating through WW1 when iron was much needed. Some of its workers served in WW1. After the war, the Foundry endured difficult times in the 1920s with industrial unrest. This continued until the late 1930s when numbers employed increased again from a low of 30 to 50 by 1938 (unpublished history, author unknown). There were other, smaller foundries in and around Eckington including one opposite Stead Street. Nail making and sickle making were long-standing local industries.

The Staveley Coal and Iron Company Ltd. also exploited the local deposits of coal and iron ironstone on the outskirts of nearby Staveley. During WW1 they began to develop their operations beyond coal tar chemicals to the production of useful-in-war chemicals such as TNT and guncotton. In various guises and majoring in chemicals the firm survived until 2012.

The Atco factory/service depot for the well-known lawnmower company was established in Eckington in the early 1920s (www.hdtrust.org). Farming, another significant industry, was partly exempted once conscription came in (see introduction to section above). Several men from the Sitwell estate served, including Will Cartlidge (see Cartlidge family). Many occupations were represented amongst Eckington's WW1 servicemen, such as motor trades, some servicemen were tradesmen such as Harry Lund who was a painter and decorator.

WOMEN AND SUFFRAGE
Women's Roles

This section will look specifically at the role of women in Eckington in WW1 and the years that followed. These were times of change and activity for women.

In the pages of the Eckington, Staveley and Woodhouse Express for the War Years to the mid 1920s and other newspapers of those times, women are virtually invisible. They were not often photographed or reported on. Most pictures were in any case ones of serving military men and occasionally others. With the very large number of men away in the military and navy, however, women had to cover their household work and in some cases work outside the home for the first time. Some, sadly, were widowed: nine of the 78 men on the Eckington War Memorial identified when our first booklet was published were known to be married. It is now clear from newspaper reports that numbers were higher. Many other families lost sons. Some war-wounded men returned to be nursed at home by wives and mothers. A proportion of these returned to the front, a significant number were permanently disabled. The 'flu epidemic of 1918 was a further nursing burden on the

women of Eckington.

In terms of work outside the home, there were areas where women had traditionally worked, for example domestic service, farming, in shops and in some metal trades (sickle making). Eckington women served in all these capacities. However, the evidence is that most women of the period in Eckington were not working outside the home. The brides in almost all of the wartime marriages in the Eckington Parish register had no recorded occupation. It is likely that women undertaking work on a formal basis was lower in Eckington than elsewhere, simply because the primary industry, coal mining, was not open to women (The Mines and Colliery Act of 1842 had prohibited women and boys under 10 from working underground) and in any case miners were exempt from call-up once conscription was introduced. Industries which employed large numbers of women in WW1 such as munitions, and transport were largely urban.

Later on in the twentieth century, more work for women developed in Eckington. The Derbyshire Canneries was established by the 1950s and went on for many decades. The workforce was largely female although the work was hard and had a number of associated conditions such as carrot rash. It meant that crops such as peas, carrots and strawberries which grew relatively locally (Derbyshire, Nottinghamshire and Lincolnshire) could be canned soon after harvesting and with relatively low transport costs.

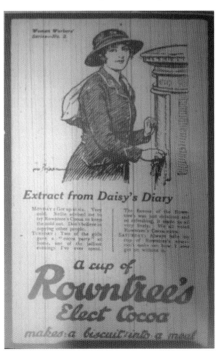

Registration

The National Registration Act, 1915, required all men and women between 15 and 65 to register for work. 15th August was Registration Day for the initial census to establish the new National Register. Information on how to apply for work was available from the Employment Exchanges which had been established under the Liberal Government in 1909.

Nursing

Nursing was one of the first occupations to employ women outside the home in any numbers. During WW1 (and also WW2), trained military nurses such as the Queen Alexandra's Royal Army Nursing Corps were supplemented by the VADs, the Voluntary Aid Detachment. In this volunteer unit, civilians who provided nursing care to military service personnel at home in the UK and abroad in stations behind the lines. 74,000 VADs were serving in 1924, two thirds reported to be women. We have no evidence that any Eckington women served in this capacity at the time of writing, beyond a picture of one local nurse tending a group of soldiers in hospital 'blues' which is known to be local (see Robinson family story).

Military Service

A small number of Eckington Women signed up for the Women's Army Auxiliary Corps. 7,000 UK women served in the Corps between 1917 and 1920. A number of Eckington women are known to have served. Three reports of women soldiers home on leave appear in the Eckington, Staveley and Woodhouse Express in 1918. The first report is of Captain Daisy Palmer, daughter of Mr and Mrs W Palmer of 3 Pot houses Eckington, was home on leave in February. She had formerly worked in Sheffield on Government Work. Daisy was engaged to a Captain J White, also of Eckington.

Miss Anne Kitteridge of Dronfield Road Eckington also served. In September, Miss Mary White, daughter of Mrs Mary White of 60 High Street, is reported as having rejoined the WAAC.

No women are memorialised on the Eckington War Memorial. Hopefully this indicates that there were no deaths. Two WW1 nurses are memorialised on the Barlborough memorial.

Fundraising and supporting the troops

Many young women were involved in the extensive fundraising activities that went on throughout WW1. To take an example from June 1918 (reported in the Eckington, Staveley and Woodhouse Express 6th July), the annual Alexandra Day collection took place in Eckington and nine local girls took part. This annual event started in 1912 and still continues nationally. It involves the sale of roses to raise money for hospitals and charities. The Honorary Secretary of the local organising committee was of course, male (Mr. Herbert Pett). Sometimes ladies would actively participate in concerts and entertainments, such as a concert at the Wesleyan Schoolroom later the same month. In August, a garden party took place in the rectory garden

for the association for entertaining
wounded soldiers. These events, one
or two a week, had the dual purpose
of entertaining local people, including
wounded soldiers and those on leave,
and fundraising.

*Harriet Ellen (Nellie) Glasby
and younger sister Emily Ida*

Suffrage and Sylvia Pankhurst

Women's suffrage was a major issue from the late 19th into the 20th Century up to 1928, when women over the age of 21 finally got the same rights to vote and to be Members of Parliament as men. The better remembered date is 1918, when some women in the UK first got the right to vote having been explicitly banned from voting by two Acts in the 1830s. The National Society for Women's Suffrage formed in 1872 had first started to press for change; the later National Union of Women's Suffrage Societies had later been more influential and finally the Women's Social and Political Union (WSPU) had started a militant campaign in 1906. This continued up to the outbreak of WW1 in 1914. Emmeline Pankhurst, leader of the WSPU and her daughter Christabel were supportive of the War and militant tactics were ceased during it. Emmeline Pankhurst's younger daughter Sylvia, was a pacifist and a socialist. Pacifism was very unpopular during the war and Sylvia was widely vilified for it.

Sylvia Pankhurst, according to her own article in 'The Workers Dreadnought: for International Socialism' Volume 5, Issue 32, dated 2nd November 1918, had made a speech to the Cresswell Labour Party on 28th September. She was

subsequently summoned to appear before the magistrates' bench at Renishaw on a charge of that she 'did unlawfully to cause mutiny, sedition, or disaffection amongst His Majesty's Forces or amongst the civilian population contrary to regulation 42 of the Defence of the Realm Regulations'. At the meeting the court was told that she had apparently said that the war 'had been the greatest crime of civilisation and was absolutely a Capitalist War. It was not a War of Freedom or Liberation. It was not a War for subject nations. It was a sordid scramble between two rival groups of capitalists who were struggling to get control of the world's raw materials.' She did not disagree with the words. The police bought forward two witnesses who said they thought the speech was objectionable. Many witnesses, including the Treasurer from the Derbyshire Miners' Association and a

Cresswell Councillor, gave evidence that the meeting was orderly and enthusiastic and that the speech was 'heard gladly'. Nevertheless, the magistrates fined her the, then very considerable sum of £50 plus £8.12 shillings costs. The alternative was 3 months imprisonment. Well-wishers raised £11 on the day with the intention of raising the full sum to avoid her committal. She planned a further speech to the Cresswell Labour Party on the 2nd November. The Magistrates Court was behind the Police Station in Renishaw. The building is still standing in Renishaw (next to what is now the Sitwell Arms Hotel) but has not functioned as either a court or a police station for many decades.

The Labour Party was developing in the early years of the 20th Century in parallel with the attempts to widen suffrage. The Independent Labour Party (ILP) was founded in 1893, when the Liberal Party appeared reluctant to endorse working class candidates and the Labour Representation Committee, soon renamed the Labour Party, was established in 1900. The two had come together in 1906 when the ILP affiliated to the Labour Party. The new party was popular in North East Derbyshire and many local towns established branches, including Eckington (meeting place the Royal Hotel during 1918) which also had a women's section by the 1920s. One of many connections between the Labour Party and the campaign for women's suffrage was that many men, especially from the working class, did not have the vote, as there was a property owning qualification. The Liberal Party led National Coalition headed by Prime Minster David Lloyd George changed this in 1918. At this point there had been no election for 8 years on account of the War, and, with the end of the War in sight there was a clear need for one. The government realised that it was timely to enfranchise non-property owning men and a proportion of women. Many of the men had been fighting (and dying) for their country whilst lacking the power to vote. The case for women to be enfranchised was also widely accepted by 1918, helped by their work and sacrifices. An editorial in the Eckington, Staveley and Woodhouse Express in February 1918, suggested that 'the female vote is quite an incalculable quantity but its main tendency should be modern and democratic'. The Representation of the People Act, now more widely remembered for enfranchising women, gave the vote to all men over 21 and women over 30 who met minimum property qualifications (most did so through their husbands). The Act extended the male electorate to 12.9 Million and introduced a new female electorate of 8.5 Million.

A new register was promptly developed in 1918 and prior to an election in December, which elected a Liberal-Conservative Government under David Lloyd George. This became known as the 'Coupon Election': the Coalition 'coupon' was a letter signed by Lloyd George on the 20th November sent to approved Coalition candidates. It was intended to demonstrate the patriotism of these candidates and promote their election. In an attempt to disparage the letter, the Liberal party leader, H H Asquith, referred to it as a 'coupon', which had negative connotations at the time on account of rationing. Whilst the Coalition succeeded in the election, the Liberal Party never recovered its former strength.

Special arrangements made in the election for military men, most of who had not been discharged, to vote. The working of the Act can be seen very clearly in the Eckington register. There were 3 sections to it (the last category too small to be of significance). The first detailed all those who qualified to vote under the occupation and property related criteria. This included 1,034 men and 724 women (42%). The majority of these women (91%) qualified through their husband's occupation. Of the men only 52 (5%) were serving in the military or navy. The second section contains 387 men, 60% of whom were in the military or navy. One family which indicates the continuing inequality of the criteria is the Sitwell Family of Renishaw Hall. The 1918 register contains the names of Sir George Reresby and Lady Ida Sitwell in Section 1. Section 2 contains the names of their sons, Osbert and Sacheverell, both at that time serving in HM Forces. Their elder sister, (later Dame) Edith Sitwell, does not appear in either section. She was at that time over 30, but was unable to meet the property criteria for women in Eckington. She may well have been registered in London if she owned property there. The Sitwell siblings were well known in London as writers at that time.

The newly enfranchised men and women were called on to vote

on three more occasions following after the election of December, 1918: in November 1922 returning a Conservative Government under Bonar Law and again in December 1923 with a minority Conservative Government under Stanley Baldwin. This collapsed in January 1924, making way for the first Labour Government of the UK, led by Ramsey Macdonald, also a minority government. A further election in October produced a Conservative Government under Stanley Baldwin. These were turbulent times.much later.

Influenza (Spanish 'Flu)

The influenza outbreak towards the end of WW1 affected both service personnel and civilians. The estimate is that 500M people were infected. It was the first global pandemic and is estimated to have been responsible for 250,000 UK deaths. Other deaths Worldwide include 18 Million in India. The name Spanish 'Flu was given to it after King Alfonso X111 of Spain fell gravely ill with it. The conditions which lead to the pandemic were first of all a new 'flu virus, H1N1, similar to but more virulent than the Swine 'Flu one of 2009. This spread fast and far because there was so much international travel resulting from troop movements. Both those in the military and support personnel and civilians were worn down by years of fighting and poor nutrition and were vulnerable. There was quite an understanding of the causes at the time; there were comments in the press that an inferior diet might be partly responsible, also people crowding together at meetings. Many more people had the 'flu than died of it, but in a minority of cases the condition worsened and became a pneumonia which killed. There was no effective cure, as continued to be the case for many decades. It is only now that there is relatively effective vaccination and also anti-biotics and

other treatments to minimise the death toll. Even so, as can be seen with the Coronavirus (Covid-19), spreading from China in 2020, measures such as quarantine and disinfection are still vital in public health moves to reduce the spread of infection. The lack of an effective cure in 1918 did not stop the manufacturers of an assortment of cough medicines, pills and potions promoting their wares, for example, Veno's Lightening Cough Cure was promoted as a 'wonderful cure' for Spanish 'flu and gas. Some drugs were effective to a degree; the then new drug, Aspirin, was helpful in reducing fever and pain and was used in large quantities. The editorial in the Eckington, Staveley and Woodhouse Express advised isolation, bed rest, good food and fresh air. Many women were involved in informal but effective community nursing (see Harriet Lund in Lund Family story).

Eckington and Renishaw, particularly Barbers Row (hamlet now demolished) were badly hit. There are reports of cases throughout 1918. Only at the very end of the year were cases said to be reducing. There were a high number of cases in June and July, with two deaths attributed to it. Barbers Row and Renishaw deaths peaked in August, with the deaths of two children and a Miss Gee, aged 18.

Harriet Ellen (Nellie) and Arthur Lund

In the peaks of the epidemic locally both the Council and Camms Schools were closed for periods of 1 week to a fortnight (the last in December 1918) as were the Methodist and Parish churches. Sergeant Major Charles E Priday, died of 'flu on Armistice Day, in hospital close to his barracks in Cannock, Staffordshire. He had served the Gloucester Regiment. An older man, with a family, his skills as a gym instructor were greatly in demand for troop training and he had been re-called to army service early in the war. He was buried in Eckington cemetery and is remembered on Eckington, Renishaw and Spinkhill memorials.

'Flu may have caused more deaths around that time than is possible to know without delving into death records. Pte Albert Rhodes died of a reported 'rapid consumption' at the home of his uncle, on Dronfield Road, Eckington, in April 1918 and is a possible 'flu casualty as are Mr A Hughes aged 56, former licensee of the Duke Hotel, Eckington who died in November after 'two weeks pneumonia' and Mrs Price, wife of William Price, Clockmaker of 89 Market Street who died the same week leaving a family of 5 children. Mrs Selima Kirk aged 52 also died at this time, leaving a widower, four sons and five daughters. She was 'well known and respected throughout the Eckington district'. Had she been nursing 'flu victims? A sad death known to have been 'flu was that of Miss Nora Thompson White, aged 16, youngest daughter of Mr and Mrs T White of Henry Street. Nora White had been a Sunday School teacher at the Wesleyan Methodist Chapel, a member of the choir and had taken part in many fund-raising concerts.

Food and Fuel

As the war progressed food became an important issue. The disruption created by the war in terms of producing food and importing it to the UK gave rise to a need to control access to it and to encourage careful use. Merchant ships were frequently attacked by German U-boats (submarines). The talk in 1917 was of 'The Food Crisis' but reluctance to introduce rationing which had not been done before. Formal rationing of food was eventually introduced in 1918, following years of exhortation to save and use food well:

Save the Wheat

and

Help the Fleet

Eat Less Bread

People were only allowed limited quantities of sugar, meat, flour, butter, tea and milk. Consumers had to register with shops which were then empowered to supply them. There were Grocers meetings to discuss how this would all work. There was competition between different shops for people to register with them for their supplies, for example, 'You must register for tea. Do so at your nearest Maypole branch'.

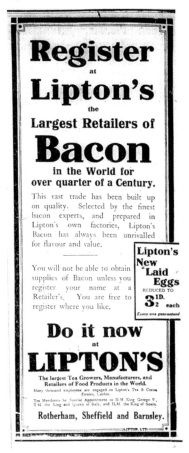

Register

at

Lipton's

the

Largest Retailers of

Bacon

in the World for
over quarter of a Century.

This vast trade has been built up on quality. Selected by the finest bacon experts, and prepared in Lipton's own factories, Lipton's Bacon has always been unrivalled for flavour and value.

You will not be able to obtain supplies of Bacon unless you register your name at a Retailer's. You are free to register where you like.

Lipton's New Laid Eggs
REDUCED TO
3½D. each

Every one guaranteed

Do it now

at

LIPTON'S

The largest Tea Growers, Manufacturers, and Retailers of Food Products in the World.

Many thousand employees are engaged on Lipton's Tea & Cocoa Estates, Ceylon.

Tea Merchants by Special Appointment to H.M. King George V., T.M. the King and Queen of Italy, and H.M. the King of Spain.

Rotherham, Sheffield and Barnsley.

LIPTON, LTD

Ironically, the previous week had reported that Pte W Robinson of the Kings own Light Yorkshire Light Infantry (KOYLI) serving in France had become a prisoner of war. He had previously worked at The India and China Tea store in Eckington.

There was also a shortage of coal as fuel which became quite extreme by 1918 and again, exhortation through advertisements was used to get people to moderate their use. An advertisement issued by the Coal Mines Department of the Board of Trade said:

Hide the Poker

Every time you poke the fire you poke away heat. You break off little chips of coal that never get burnt at all. And you take out or push through the bars some of the living coal, so that you decrease the heat of the fire instead of increasing it, as you imagine.

And the proof of it is that you will, if you watch, almost always see that anyone who pokes the fire immediately puts on more coal. In fact,

Hundreds of thousands of tons of coal per year would be saved if all the pokers in the country were put away.

Think what this means to you. It means the saving of many scuttles full of coal. It means an extra fire just at the moment you need it most. Get rid of the poker to-day.

A COAL POKER IS A COAL WASTER

Issued by the Coal Mines Dept., Board of Trade, Holborn Viaduct, E.C.1.
B.T.16.

Growing food locally became a feature of life and for many years during the war and after, the Eckington, Staveley and Woodhouse Express had an allotments column explaining how best to manage them, what to plant when etc. In March 1918, an allotments feature reported that a federation was to be formed. The same edition carried an advertisement on behalf of Lord Rhondda and Mr Prothero exhorting every man who has a farm, a garden or an allotment to plant more potatoes, to make Yorkshire self-sufficient in what was grown and consumed, an additional 91,000 tons. One month later, Eckington Gossip reported that a large number of allotments had been thrown open for cultivation. There was a problem with potato disease in 1918 and such was the importance of the crop, that the Parish Council held a special meeting.

In 1917, the Local Government Board had decided that local authorities were to be asked to encourage pig rearing but not in congested areas.

Housing

There was a growing concern through the war years that the UK's housing was substandard and that there was a shortage. The last years of the war in particular, provided an opportunity to consider the problem and make plans for addressing it after the War. Throughout 1917, the Eckington Staveley and Woodhouse Express ran a series of eight articles by experts on housing issues and their thinking for the future, entitled 'Healthy Housing'. In the first, Lord Henry Bentinck explained that top issues were emigration and slums. The two were connected; if housing was poor and there were insufficient homes, families would be tempted to emigrate, depriving the country of its young workforce. He said that the first step would be for the State to recognise its responsibility. In the second article in August 1917, B Seebolm Rowntree put forward the radical idea that housing did not need to be near work. This was in the context of the rapid urbanisation of the country through the Nineteenth Century. Whilst not traditionally urban, Eckington had a poor record for housing with much of it in bad condition. Two cases of typhoid in a housing court in the centre of the village from the Nightingale family (one young man of the two victims died) illustrates some of the conditions experienced. Many parts of Eckington were very unpleasant. At a Parish Council meeting early in 1918 it was alleged that 'refuse lies in heaps in yards and that these apply in hundreds of cases.' Families at this time tended to be large at all levels of society. Joseph Wells had 13 children. Working families also had large families; religion, lack of reliable birth control, child mortality and a wish to have children to support parents in old age were all contributory factors. During the war, it was a mark of honour for families to have many sons in military service. Mrs Crawford of 85 Market Street, Eckington was reported as having seven sons at the Front. At the level of the working man, there was overcrowding in many homes.

Cleanliness would be a difficult issue too with many people working in collieries, ironworks and farming. Bessie Harrop's father was a miner and exempted from War Service in WW1. He worked first at Barlborough Colliery and later at West-thorpe. For him conditions for the miners improved during WW2 when they had the towels and soap and washing facilities. Miners at the time of WW1 were without such basics and the tin bath would be a feature in many homes. Cleaning clothes was also an issue. From the advertisements during the war years, women would also be expected to wash the kit of those home on leave.

In May 1918 The National Housing Scheme was unveiled. The President of the Local Government

Board was in discussions about addressing the 'Housing crisis' by building 200,000 'Labourers' Cottages' across the country. Eligible candidates would have to be paying National Insurance. Building was expected to start immediately demobilisation began. In 1919 the Government passed the ambitious Addison Act, named after Christopher Addison, the then Minister of Health and Housing. It promised subsidies to help the construction of 500,000 houses in the three years after the war. It recognised a national duty for housing and gave local authorities the responsibility for developing plans for housing and ensuring that it was built, for rent where necessary. It was the start of council, now social housing.

Nationally, less than half the houses were ever built. Eckington really only benefitted from the new schemes after WW2, when the large Birk Hill and Castle Hill Estates were built. In the much harder financial conditions of the 1920s and with two of the major collieries closed – Renishaw Park and Hornthorpe (see mining), Eckington expanded very little after WW1. A few additional houses were built but little slum clearance took place until much later. Those that were built by the local authority between the Wars were in central Eckington. Street names favoured Labour politicians (Hardie, Lansbury) and Royalty (Edward, Mary).

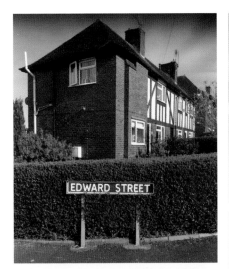

FAMILY
Nightingale

Informant: David Nightingale, grandson of John Tom and Ethel Nightingale

This extended family is very typical of many in Eckington at the time of WW1. The family had first established itself in the town as a result of Jeremiah Nightingale's experience as a Staffordshire nailmaker. He had come to North East Derbyshire in 1765 with his wife Martha, and by 1770 was established in Eckington with the first three of their children. By the beginning of the 20th Century there were several Nightingale households established in the town, some in neighbouring properties in the Fanshaw Road area. John Tom and Ethel Alice Nightingale, David Nightingale's grandparents at No. 13 Fanshaw Road and the older family of Charles and Agnes Nightingale at No. 10.

Charles was the eldest son of William Nightingale, who had followed the family trade of nailmaking. His long life had ended just before the start of WW1 in November 1913 and was covered by the Derbyshire Times. The paper noted that at 88, William Nightingale had been one of the oldest inhabitants of the Parish of Eckington. Two of his brothers had also lived to over 80 and his father to the very great age for those times of 95. Charles inherited number 10 from his father. He worked as a carter. In 1911 the family had experienced tragedy when Charles' son, Alwyn, aged 22 died in dramatic circumstances in an carting accident at the corner of Fanshaw Road with West Road. The horse had bolted and as it veered between a house and a lamp post, the cart was smashed and Alwyn was thrown out to his death.

John Tom was the son of William's second wife. Like his neighbouring half-brother, John Tom worked with horses, in his case as an Ostler (stableman) who looked after the pit horses at the nearby Hornthorpe Colliery. This picture is John Tom in old age with a pony, Shanty.

He was also a pigeon fancier; this is a picture of him as a younger man with his two sons, William (elder boy) and Walter Albert, David's father.

Other Nightingale families lived elsewhere in Eckington. The Derbyshire Times reported in February 1906 that a young man named Thomas Nightingale aged 23 had been removed to isolation hospital from 43 Church Street suffering from typhoid, his brother James survived. The disease had originated in Northgate, where defective drainage was held responsible for the outbreak and was to be improved.

Arthur Nightingale died in October 1916 at the age of 21. He was the son of James and Ellen Nightingale. It was a second tragedy for that family; an earlier-born son, named Arthur had died in childhood. Pte Edgar Nightingale, was his four year older first cousin. He had enlisted at the beginning of the war and by 1918 he was married and living at 124 High Street, a short distance from 2 Fanshaw Road where he was born. He died on the 20th August, following a second gas attack but on this occasion he was also hit by a shell. Weeks earlier, on the 20th July, a half uncle, James Thomas Barker, also serving with the Sherwood Foresters, died in Cologne.

Another first cousin of Arthur and Edgar survived the war. James Nightingale, was serving in the regular army at the outbreak of war and was sent to serve in WW1 in 1914. By 1918 he was a well-known figure in Eckington. He acted as Master of Ceremonies to a dance held in the Assembly Rooms, Eckington, in November 1918 in support of the National Association of Discharged Soldiers. It seems likely that James himself was discharged through injury at some point during the war.

Nellie Nightingale, daughter of Charles and Agnes Nightingale at No. 10 Fanshaw Road, was a cousin once removed of Edgar and Arthur. In April 1918 she had a 'pretty wedding' to William Chambers of Barrowhill. The year was a happier and more forward- looking year than 1916 or 1917. Hopes of peace seemed higher; the overall number of deaths in Eckington had reduced from the 27 of 1917 to 16 by the end of the year. The number of marriages (based on the number solemnised in the Parish Church, although not all were) had returned to 57, following a 1917 low of 42. Nellie and William Chambers were given a house, the Laurels, on Chesterfield Road as a wedding present from Nellie's parents. The Laurels, with its recognisable Edwardian style, is still standing today.

13 Fanshaw Road was later to become the first marital home of Mavis Hume (nee Fisher). Mavis and her sister Janet are the daughters of Joseph Fisher (born 1910) who was a miner and granddaughters of Joseph Fisher who served in the navy in WW1. Joseph (senior) had returned from the war and typically for the times, never wished to talk about his experiences. He returned to his work as a miner. Also a miner, his son Joseph (junior) was exempt from service in WW2.

EPLIOGUE

World War 1, the Great War, was sometimes called the 'war to end wars'. It proved not to be, even for the Western European powers. It was certainly the one with the greatest death toll, especially for the UK. It saw a number of firsts, none of them happy: the first to use modern weapons, chemical warfare, war in the air, and involvement of civilians at home. It changed state boundaries and the balance of world power, seeing the end of the Austro-Hungarian Empire and a rise in the significance of the USA. It led to the establishment of the League of Nations which later became the United Nations. It pushed on progress on a number of fronts; the modern role and emancipation of women, better working conditions, better housing, rapid communications and greater travel. It led to improvements in medicine and nursing.

It deeply affected the lives of a great many people: those who lost their lives, never fulfilling the promise they had; those who served and returned with their memories; and those who lost family members. Even now, a large proportion of the UK population living has a grandfather or great grandfather who served, or a great uncle who died. Remembrance has been strong and lasting in the case of this war. Hopefully this book will be a source of information to current and later residents of Eckington who want to explore the history of the men and their families through the war and afterwards into the 1920s.

REFERENCE SOURCES AND SELECTED BIBLIOGRAPHY

Eckington, Staveley and Woodhouse Express 1914-1924 editions (held on microfiche, Chesterfield Library)

Renishaw & Spinkhill WW1 and WW2 Project, Ed. Richard Godley, 2019

The Quick and The Dead, Fallen Soldiers and Their Families in the Great War, Richard Van Emden, Bloomsbury, 2012

The Platoon: An Infantryman on the Western Front 1916-1918 John Jones Steward Eds. Andrew Robertshaw and Steve Roberts Pen & Sword Military, 2011

The Coal Mining Industry of Sheffield and North Derbyshire, Ken Wain, Amberley Publishing, 2014

WW1: Eckington Soldiers and their Families: Commemorating their Sacrifice on the 100th Anniversary of the Armistice, November 2018 (Reference copies in local libraries), 2018

9th Service Battalion: The Sherwood Foresters: Notts and Derby Regiment during the First World War, John Stephen Morse, Tommies Guides, 2007.

The names of the 85 WW1 fallen on the Eckington War Memorial are listed in the annual tables of war dead in the Timeline section of this book and alphabetically with military service information in the companion booklet, WW1: Eckington Soldiers and their Families: Commemorating their Sacrifice on the centenary of the Armistice, 2018.